THE LUATH GUIDES

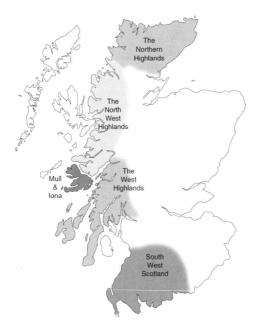

South West Scotland

The West Highlands: the Lonely Lands

Mull & Iona: Highways & Byways

The North West Highlands: Roads to the Isles

The Northern Highlands: the Empty Lands

Mull & Iona:
Highways & Byways

PETER MACNAB

Luath Press Limited

EDINBURGH

www.luath.co.uk

First Edition 1986
Reprinted 1987
Revised Edition 1988
New Edition 1990
Reprinted 1991
Revised Edition 1992
Revised Edition 1993
New Edition 1994
Revised Edition 1995
Revised Edition 1996
Revised Edition 1997
Reprinted 1997
Reprinted 1998
Revised Edition 1999
Reprinted 2003

The paper used in this book is acid-free, neutral-sized and recyclable.
It is made from low-chlorine pulps produced in a low-energy,
low-emission manner from sustainable forests.

Printed and bound by
Bell & Bain Ltd., Glasgow

Maps by Jim Lewis

Illustrations by Anthony Fury

Typeset in 10.5 point Sabon by
Senga Fairgrieve, Edinburgh, 0131 658 1763

A message from the Publishers

Our authors welcome feedback from their readers, so do please let us have your comments and suggestions. The feedback we have received indicates that the Luath Guides are valued by their readers and that their usefulness is enhanced by the inclusion of advertisements for local businesses whose support Luath Press greatly appreciates. We, in turn, encourage our readers to make use of their products and services. Mention Luath Press when you do. The author's editorial independence is unaffected by the inclusion of these advertisements.

Whilst we make every effort to ensure that information in our books is correct, we can accept no responsibility for any accident, loss or inconvenience arising.

Index Map

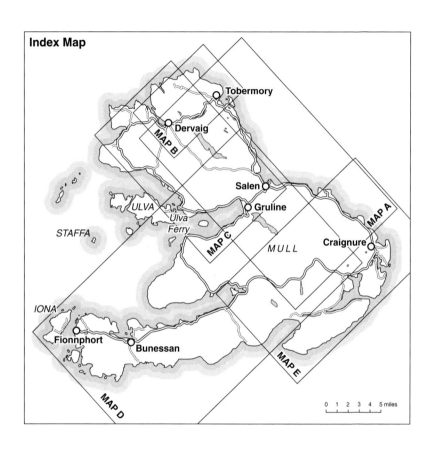

Tobermory

Dervaig

MAP B

Salen

ULVA

Gruline

STAFFA

Ulva Ferry

MAP C

Craignure

MAP A

MULL

IONA

Fionnphort

Bunessan

MAP E

MAP D

0 1 2 3 4 5 miles

Contents

Foreword

Royal Mail is committed to providing mail services to communities throughout Scotland.

As part of our commitment to rural communities, Royal Mail runs a network of postbus services – mail vehicles which carry passengers as well as mail and provide a valuable service in areas where no other public transport exists. These services are used both by local people and by tourists travelling throughout Scotland. Postbus timetables are available from local tourist offices.

In this, the National Year of Reading in Scotland, Royal Mail is delighted to support this series of Luath Guides written by people who have a thorough knowledge of the area and an enthusiasm to share a love of Scotland with their readers.

Please enjoy reading them as you travel around Scotland.

Alex Gibb

Alex Gibb
Director and General Manager
Royal Mail Scotland & Northern Ireland

Introduction

The Isle of Mull is of Isles the fairest,
Of ocean's gems 'tis the first and rarest;
Green grassy island of sparkling fountains,
Of waving woods and high tow'ring mountains.

THESE WORDS ARE AS TRUE today as when they were written over one hundred years ago by the great Mull bard Dugald MacPhail, when he was working in Newcastle, far from his homeland.

As a visitor to Mull and Iona, you will naturally want to know something about the islands before setting out to explore their highways and byways. Here, in this little book, you will find not only items of interest common to all the Hebridean islands, but also certain features unique to the two islands of Mull and Iona.

From the earliest times, Mull, the third largest of the Hebridean islands, has been the social and strategic centre of the southern Hebrides. It flanks the Firth of Lorne, where the trans-Scotland line of communications along the Great Glen opens to the sea in the west. In the days when land communication was difficult and dangerous, this almost continuous waterway was one of the very few means of contact between the west and the east of Scotland. Mainland Oban, which was called the 'Charing Cross of the Highlands' when the railway came more than one hundred years ago, lies only ten miles distant across the Firth. The sheltered Sound of Mull, with the mainland of Morvern and Ardnamurchan to the north, leads to Tobermory Bay, the finest harbour in the Hebrides, where dozens of ships, many far-travelled, used to call or shelter in past years; today it is a yachts-man's paradise. No wonder Mull of the Mountains was and still is a natural focal point.

Geologically, Mull is one of the most thoroughly researched areas of the world. Basically, it is a portion of the West Highland mainland cut off by ages of erosion, then – except for Iona and the tip of the Ross of Mull – covered up and depressed under thousands of feet of successive piled-up lava sheets that flowed from a great central volcano, from lesser vents and from a network of fissures in the land surface.

During the last thirty to forty million years the agents of erosion have worn away vast masses of rock. The sea has cut into the softer rocks, leaving long sea lochs with bold headlands of harder rocks; glens were deepened and smoothed by glaciers. The last of the ice disappeared 10/12,000 years ago, depositing the isolated boulders, the heaps of glacial detritus, the ice-scored rock surfaces we see today, some of the rocks having been carried by the ice from far up the Great Glen. Prominent, too, are the raised beaches which can be traced for miles along the coast, which mark the slow rise of the land as it was relieved of its weight of ice. Now we can see along the slopes of the hills and glens the cut-back edges of the successive lava flows, with a skyline like steps and stairs, especially in north-west Mull.

It was not only the strategic situation of Mull, but also its fertile soil and green grassy hills that attracted settlers from earliest pre-history. The presence of over forty forts and defensive structures along the south and west coasts points to the resistance put up by earlier settlers to the later waves of perhaps more warlike Celts from Ireland, when Mull became an influential part of the ancient kingdom of Dalriada.

Mull's later castles remind us of the powerful clans MacDonald and Maclean who ruled the southern Hebrides. Aros Castle, near Salen, on the Sound of Mull, and Ardtornish, on the Morvern shore opposite, were the principal seats of the Lords of the Isles, princes whose might rivalled, and indeed often threatened, that of the king himself in Edinburgh.

Sadly, evil times came with the nineteenth century. In 1821 there was an expanding, self-supporting population of about 10,000 in Mull and 500 in Iona. By the end of the century those figures were reduced to 4,500 and 150, and were steadily falling.

This destruction of a way of life was the responsibility of a new generation of landowners, frequently, although not invariably, newly rich industrialists from England, who had 'bought' the land from the degenerate clan chiefs, stripped now of their traditional powers by the political aftermath of the '45 uprising, often apeing the social life of the South, and in so doing becoming so desperate for cash that some of them became the most directly responsible for horrific clearances, rocketing rents, poverty, exploited emigration, and the end of the Clan System, which at its height has been described as 'The finest example of benevolent feudalism in Europe.' Protected by smug Victorian privilege, their treatment of a simple trusting people, who had no legal redress, was unforgiveable and unforgettable, even more in the case of the remote central government for its indifference and hypocrisy. While bravely putting down slavery abroad, it was ignoring such evils as the Clearances at home, while forcing opium on the Chinese literally at cannon point.

The sad story of the Clearances is well documented and Mull had more than its share. In fact, if we analyse official records, it would appear that some lairds even took pride in cunningly outwitting a trusting community, as in the north of Mull, and showed sheer cruelty in the case of the island of Ulva. Some of the indifference on the part of southerners came from a traditional contempt for Highlanders. During the Napoleonic Wars, the Prime Minister, William Pitt, is reported to have said 'I have found a new use for Highlanders: they make good cannon fodder.'

Destitution became so widespread in the area centring on Mull that the Mull Combination Poorhouse, as it was called, was built in 1862 at a convenient spot near Tobermory. It had accommodation for up to 100 to 130 homeless people. It was built and maintained by a consortium of parishes, at public expense, of course, and managed by a committee consisting mostly of the very landowners who had brought about the need for such an institution by their policy of clearances and the introduction of sheep. It was demolished in the 1970s.

It is true that in some areas a measure of depopulation was necessary, for with an increasing population the sub-division of crop-lands had brought a risk of real poverty. The evil lay in the manner in which this was forced upon the people. After the Clearances, sheep grazed among the ruined homesteads. The writer recalls that when he was a boy, an old man told him that when he was about the same age, his father carried him out of the cottage built by his forefathers, and outside the factor was waiting with a blazing torch to burn it to the ground. This happened on the island of Ulva, where the population of 500 dropped to 200 in ten years.

Anyway, in time, over-grazing by sheep fouled the land, despoiling it of the fertility built up over the centuries by mixed, chiefly cattle, agriculture, and the land was taken over by rabbits and bracken, finally reverting to barren sporting estates. Mull was no longer the fine cattle country it had been.

The visitor will notice how good land is still slowly vanishing under conifers. There is a sheep instead of a cattle economy, and a system of doles and grants handed out by a government more interested in catering to Big Industry, while keeping the economy of Mull barely ticking over. Mull, in fact, has been described as a microcosm of the whole Highlands problem. It shares with the other islands the disadvantages of high freights for the carriage of goods, and at least ten pence more on a gallon of petrol than in Oban, where the price is already much higher than in the south. With so few public services, Mull is entirely dependent on the motor car. Subsidies to equate the price of petrol to that on the mainland, and equating freight charges to road transport costs (Roads Equivalent Tariff) could well transform the economy of Mull and that of the other islands. Such subsidies would hardly be noticed in the national budget, although of course even the idea of action of that sort is anathema in the present political climate.

Since ferry communications and new standards of living were introduced in the 1950s and '60s, Mull has become an increasingly popular holiday island with a vast choice of interests and accommodation. Unfortunately, tourism is a precarious industry depending on many factors, few of them under the control of the people directly concerned.

But the great event in Mull's social history was its close association with Iona and St Columba, which is described in a later Chapter. The radiance emanating from what has been called 'the morning star of Scotland's faith' was shed not only over Mull, but over Scotland, north-east England, Scandinavia (through the later Vikings), and even into Europe along the Rhine Valley. The practical, dedicated, militant monks of Iona, besides their learning and carrying of the Word to a pagan land, taught the crafts of building and carving, agriculture, and even the science of herbal medicine, which was taught by the famous Beaton family, generations of whom conducted a veritable health service from Mull throughout the Hebrides, when they were medical advisors to the households of the great chiefs of Mull. Late in the sixteenth century their skill was recognised even by the King of Scotland in distant Edinburgh.

Scattered over Mull there are the ruins of at least fourteen pre-Reformation chapels, which gives some indication of the influence of Iona on the social life of the people. In fact, it was the influence of Iona and its surroundings that kept civilisation alive during the dark days of lawlessness and bloodshed in Scotland.

But let us come back to today. Here in Mull you will be welcomed by a quiet, proud people, although under the veneer of modern sophistication you may sense something of the old, unhappy far-off things in the deserted ruins and bracken-infested countryside of this picturesque island. What can Mull offer to attract and interest the visitor? As Tennyson said, 'The old order changeth, yielding place to new...'

There is something of interest going on throughout the season starting with the popular Mull Festival of Music in early Spring and running through to the spectacular Mull Car Rally in October, which attracts competitors from all over Britain. In between there are the Tobermory Highland Games, the Clyde-to-Tobermory yacht race and the Mull and Morvern Agriculture Show. There are frequent ceilidh-concerts; there is the famous Mull Little Theatre in Dervaig where there is also a very interesting exhibition on Mull past and present in The Old Byre. There is a Summer School of Painting, Sheep Dog trials, Ploughing Matches, Clay Pigeon shoots, displays of local crafts – all are available – and what about a trip on the only railway in the Hebrides, between Craignure and Torosay Castle?

The sportsman will find golf at Tobermory, Craignure and Iona. For the angler, there is salmon and sea-trout fishing available and a wide choice of brown and rainbow trout waters. The sea angler will find the best sea angling in Europe centred on Tobermory although he may have to book a year ahead. There is pony trekking and stalking.

Then, for those so minded, the geology, geography, archaeology and botany of Mull are fascinating: bird-watching is very much worthwhile, and do not forget the local cruises to places of interest. There is plenty of information to be had from the local Oban and Mull Information Centre in Tobermory, and of course from local contacts.

Mull is reached by two regular roll-on, roll-off car ferries, the main one from Oban to Craignure (forty five minutes) and the other from Lochaline in Morvern to Fishnish, near Craignure (fifteen minutes), from the east and north respectively. In the summer there is a ferry, for cars and passengers, that runs between Kilchoan, in Ardnamurchan, and Tobermory. This opens up the possibility of spending some time in Ardnamurchan, and still getting back to Mull in the evening. A local bus connects Iona and Tobermory with the ferry terminus at Craignure. However, once again the EU has interfered, apparently unopposed, in our purely local affairs. As a result of a change ordered in the crews' working conditions, some confusion has been created in the 1999 season in communications and the already hard-pressed economy of the Hebrides. This involves not only sailings, but travelling connections between Caledonian-MacBrayne, Scotrail, and the City Link bus service from Glasgow. Before arranging a visit to Mull, contact Cal-Mac at Gourock Pier; advance car bookings on the Oban to Craignure service are essential. Caledonian-MacBrayne, Head Office Administration, The Ferry Terminal, Gourock, phone: 01475 650100.

Mull is ideal walking or hiking country. The author suggests Tobermory, Dervaig, Salen and Bunessan as excellent centres. Whether by roads, paths or hill tracks, there is an infinite variety, as the readers of this book will find. It is suggested that walkers of all ages should carry a stout stick: it is like a third leg over rough ground, as well as a crude but useful camera support. As a matter of fact, there are some fine makers of crooks and sticks in Mull, with winter classes held in that fascinating hobby.

Travelling from the south, or from Edinburgh, motorists may well consider taking the M8 motorway by Glasgow airport to Greenock and Gourock, thence by car ferry (20 minutes) across the Firth of Clyde to Dunoon, and on by an excellent, quiet and scenic road running past lovely Loch Eck and Loch Fyne to Inveraray, joining the Oban road at Dalmally. This avoids the often wearisome road by Loch Lomond, which, even now that so many and such expensive changes have been made, can still be a dangerous bottleneck in the height of the season.

In Mull, the motorist will have to observe extra courtesy and patience. Apart from the modernised road from Salen and Craignure to Iona Ferry, Mull roads are narrow, with passing places, steep gradients, blind corners and narrow bridges. Watch your mirror, and give way in time, using passing places for over-taking and being overtaken. Beware of cattle and sheep on unfenced roads. They can move suddenly and unpredictably, with dire results if a motorist is taken unawares – to say nothing about the financial loss to struggling sheep farmers. Of course, there are a number of places which, even though they are on a public road, are best approached on foot. Very narrow roads with bad surfaces, total lack of off-the-road parking, shortage of turning spaces and other problems mean that it is simply not worth while trying to take a car (or, worse, a caravan) to such places. Better to leave your vehicle at some convenient and safe place, and walk to where you want to go – you will find that not only will it be much less frustrating, but that you will positively enjoy the walk. And, above all, do take all your rubbish home with you. There is no garbage collection in many of the isolated places on the islands, and you really should not expect the inhab-itants to clean up after you.

The 'menace of the midge' (*Culicoedes Impunctatus*) is rather exaggerated. Oh, yes, in dull windless weather, especially in July and August, midges can be a nuisance, but the least breeze blows them away. Deterrent creams as used by Forestry workers can be effective for an hour or two. Tobacco smoke, especially that from a good-going pipeful of black twist, can help, but I have achieved complete immunity, even when fishing by the most midge-infest-ed, boggy lochside, by the inelegant medium of a very fine nylon net, green coloured, tucked well in between hat and neck. It does not interfere unduly with visibility.

Clegs and the ordinary house fly can also be a pest in hot summer weather. They can be discouraged by the example of the

Australian swagman – an old broad-brimmed hat with corks suspended round the brim on short lengths of nylon gut. The nimbus of flies must be flustered and frustrated. Again, I use this method. Who cares about appearances?

Now, don't believe the stories of Mull's super midges: even Para Handy's description in The Vital Spark of the Dervaig midges is just a little exaggerated. He told how the old ones sent youngsters into the tents of campers to test the blood groups, having first shown them the proper grip. If the blood was the right sort, then the old timers would follow up for a real feast. There has been some confirmation, though, of the super-midge which landed on Glenforsa airstrip, and was filled up with 20 gallons of fuel before anyone recognised it for a midge and not a plane.

All these pests are confined to lower ground, especially damp areas. The hill tops and upper reaches are free, and in any case there is usually a light cooling breeze there. It is worth noting that it has been estimated than when climbing the hills, the temperature drops one degree for every 300 feet of ascent; so if you are climbing Ben More, for instance, there can be a difference of 10 degrees between sea level and the summit. That is why people are advised to carry an extra pullover when climbing, even in summer.

Peter Angus Macnab

Using this Book

THE READER IS TAKEN ON a conducted tour of Mull, based on the road system, with Craignure – the car ferry terminus – as starting and finishing points. The road system is divided into five sections (A to E), and for each a sketch map is provided, marked in miles. Every place or object of interest is marked by a circled number to correspond with the numbered paragraphs in the text that follows, where there are useful cross references.

MAP A – *Craignure – Salen – Tobermory (22 miles).*

Diversions from Salen along Glen Road to Dervaig (12 miles) and from Tobermory to Glengorm (4 miles).

MAP B – *Tobermory to Dervaig* (8 miles).

MAP C – *Dervaig – Calgary – Torloisk – Ulva Ferry – Salen (Gruline) (26 miles).*

Diversion from Dervaig to Torloisk by hill road (5 miles) and from Penmore Mill to Croig (1 1/2 miles).

MAP D – *Salen (Gruline) – Gribun – Kilfinichen Church – Kinloch – Fionnphort (for Iona) (38 miles).*

Diversion from Kilfinichen Church to Tiroran (for Burg and the Fossil Tree) (6 miles).

Diversion from Pennyghael to Carsaig (4 miles).

Diversions from Bunessan and Fionnphort – various: Fossil Leaf beds, granite quarries, Erraid (David Balfour's island), cliff forts, crofting villages, beaches, and, above all, the ferry to Iona.

MAP E – *Return to Kinloch Inn – Kinloch – Glenmore – Ardura – Lochdonhead – Craignure (20 miles).*

Diversion from Ardura to Lochbuie (8 miles).

Diversion from Lochdonhead to Grass Point (old ferry terminus) (3 miles).

Diversion from Kilpatrick to Duart Castle (3 miles).

Useful Information

PETROL. Watch your petrol gauge, for filling stations are far between, in fact, non-existent in north-west Mull. You can fill up at the following places: Craignure, Salen, Tobermory, Pennyghael and Ardfenig (Bunessan).

GARAGES AND REPAIR SERVICES. Craignure, Salen, Ardefenig (Bunessan) and Tobermory, where there are excellent modern facilities.

BANKS. There is a busy branch of the Clydesdale Bank in Tobermory, and its mobile bank provides service throughout the island.

LOCAL INFORMATION. The reader will find but little detailed information in this book about general services, or such well-known places as Tobermory, Duart Castle etc. This will be found in specialised brochures. Queries will be answered and holiday accommodation arranged by the Tourist Board Offices in Oban, Tobermory and Craignure (telephone 01631 563122, 01688 302182 and 01680 812377 respectively).

POST OFFICES AND TELEPHONES. There are Post Offices with one collection and delivery daily, at Craignure, Salen, Tobermory, Dervaig, Ulva Ferry, Tiroran, Pennyghael, Bunessan, Fionnphort, Iona, Lochbuie and Lochdon. The telephone system on Mull is adequate, and has been completely modernised.

MAPS. It will be found useful to choose from the following as fill-in for the five road maps included in the text. The current one-inch

Ordnance Survey maps covering Mull are Sheets 47, 48 and 49 (1: 50,000); Bartholomew's Contoured Map of Great Britain (1: 100,000). No.47 (Mull and Oban) includes Mull and all its islands. Sheets 43 and 44 of the Geological Survey one-inch maps cover Western Mull and Central and Eastern Mull respectively.

FINALLY: Don't forget your camera, and have plenty of film. You will need it all!

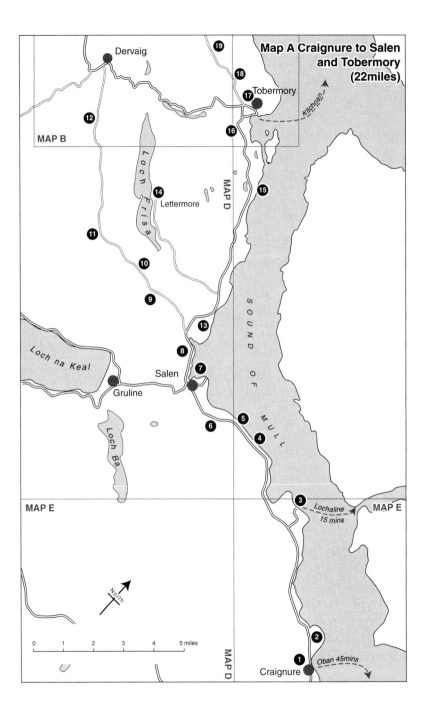

Map A Craignure to Salen and Tobermory (22miles)

Dervaig

MAP B

Tobermory

Kilchoan

Loch Frisa

Lettermore

MAP D

SOUND OF MULL

Loch na Keal

Salen

Gruline

Loch Ba

MAP E

MAP E

Lochaline
15 mins

Craignure

Oban 45mins

North

0   1   2   3   4   5 miles

MAP D

Craignure – Salen – Tobermory
(22 miles)

YOUR FIRST INTRODUCTION TO the island occurs before you set foot on it! Halfway across the Firth of Lorne on your 40 minutes' ferry trip the ship will pass through the Channel between picturesque Lismore lighthouse and to your left a tidal reef known as the Lady Rock. Here you will cross a tide-race where the tides of the Sound of Mull meet those of the Atlantic flowing up the Firth of Lorne. This is the Tide Race of the Dirks, from a very old story handed down from the 15th century when two men stabbed each other to death in an argument on how best to steer a galley.

On the Lady Rock, in the 17th century, Lachlan Catanach, described as The Only Bad Chief of Duart, marooned an unwanted wife, Elizabeth, daughter of the Duke of Argyll, leaving it to the rising tide to create an unfortunate 'accident'. Unknown to Duart, she was rescued by fishermen and duly returned to her infuriated father the Duke. She was revenged soon after when her brother stabbed the faithless Duart to death.

A1. CRAIGNURE

Craignure is now the main ferry link (See A3) between Mull and the mainland at Oban. There is the principal tourist office, an inn, Post Office, shop, garage, tea room and the nearby modern Isle of Mull Hotel, with its fine outlook. Connecting buses run to Tobermory and Iona, and there are special touring buses. The pier was built in 1962 and adapted for roll-on roll-off traffic in the early 1970s.

Turn right for Tobermory at the pierhead and proceed north-west with the long ridge of Dun Da Ghaoithe (2,512 feet) high above to the left and the blue Sound of Mull to the right. The unpronounceable name of this hill means in English 'The Hill of the Two Winds', and is so called because at the top the wind is diverted in all directions by the shape of the ridge.

Before setting out on the recommended circuit of the island, the visitor should perhaps see Torosay Castle, which lies just a mile and a half in the other direction beside the road to Iona. Its many attractions are described elsewhere (MAP E13).

After four years of voluntary work, a miniature railway was completed in 1983 and now runs between Craignure and Torosay Castle (see MAP E13).

A2. CRAIGNURE GOLF CLUB

About one mile from Craignure look right beside the new road and you will see the tiny clubhouse near the shore on the south corner of Scallastle Bay. In 1978 it was decided to re-open and re-model the nine hole golf course on the machair land here, 2,565 yards in length, Standard Scratch Score 65. It was one of the little courses opened in Mull when golf fever hit the island early in the century. In addition to Tobermory, there were 6-hole courses at Calgary and

25

Glengorm, and 9-hole courses at Salen and Craignure, as well as on Iona. Apart from the course at Iona, only Tobermory survived, and still flourishes as the Western Isles Golf Club. The course at Craignure, with possibilities of extension, is an asset to the island.

A3. FISHNISH FERRY

Five miles north of Craignure a signpost to the right indicates the mile-long road through the Forestry plantations to Fishnish Bay. This is the second of Mull's three regular car ferries to the mainland (A1), and it carries a maximum of twelve cars on the fifteen minutes' crossing to Lochaline (no advance booking is required) on the Morvern shore of the Sound of Mull. From there a good road leads from Loch Sunart to Ardgour (28 miles), where the short Corran Ferry links up with the road to Fort William (9 miles) and Oban (26 miles).

Grave slabs in Pennygown

A4. PENNYGOWN CHAPEL

To the right of the new road about nine miles from Craignure, this is one of the 14 or 15 pre-Reformation Chapels built on the island by the missionaries of Iona, and dates from the 12th century. Note the simple grave slabs inside, the piscina recess in the east wall, the highly ornamented shaft of a small broken cross, and outside, the stone steps leading from the old road, designed to exclude cattle from the cemetery, and, finally, two very old carved grave slabs at the south-east corner outside the chapel (A17, C17, D10). They are said to cover 'the only bad chief of the Duart Macleans and his wife.' As they had supposedly dabbled in witchcraft (for instance, calling up the Evil One by roasting live cats!) they were denied interment in the holy ground of the chapel, but were buried as near to it as possible.

Within the chapel walls there is the broken shaft of a fine Celtic Cross with carvings of great delicacy and beauty. According to tradition, the chapel never had a roof, through the malevolent spells of the witches who once haunted the nearby 'fairy mound'. The same tradition holds in connection with St Columba's first church in Iona, when he was obliged to inter one of his disciples (St Oran) underneath the foundations before the structure could be completed.

While on the subject, could I add that up to the 17th century, when alleged witches were cruelly burned at the stake, their interment afterwards at crossroads was in fact an act of final compassion by the Church, which, denying them interment in holy ground, allowed them to be buried at a crossroads, which by its cruciform design was held to be self-consecrated. The

A5. GLENFORSA AIRSTRIP

Two miles short of Salen, and well signposted, beyond the driveway leading to the Glenforsa Hotel, lies Mull's only airstrip. The hotel itself is unique, being of Norwegian design, looking out to the airstrip, which until 1979 was in regular use between Glasgow and Mull, about 40 minutes' flight. Except for private use, a public service was discontinued through lack of safety precautions in difficult terrain. Grass over gravel, 3,000ft by 90ft, it was built in 1966 as an exercise by the 38th Engineer Regiment.

This is the locality of the 'Great Mull Air Mystery', when early on Christmas morning in 1975 a man, Gibbs, took off alone in a hired private plane. While the plane was never seen again, his body was found four months later on a hill slope above the hotel. Both the fate of the plane and the peculiar circumstances surrounding the finding of the body and its cause of death remain a mystery.

A6. CACHALLY

This farmhouse lies a few hundred yards north of A5. Here were found relics of the Bronze Age, sepulchral urns, pottery sherds, flint blades, bronze fragments and portions of an ancient beaker.

A7. SALEN *('The Salty Place')*

The village was built about 1800 by General Lachlan Macquarie, 'Father of Australia' (see D1). It is a busy village, a centre of the road system, with shops, Post Office (officially 'Aros'), garages and hotels. The word *Aros* is from the Scandinavian, meaning an estuary e.g. Aarhus, in Denmark. Behind the hotel in the centre of the village there is a rocky bluff from which St Columba is said to have addressed a congregation. It was 'not very well attended', we are still told. A tiny burn whose name means 'The Burn of the Sermons' flows nearby. There are traces of a chapel further up, which is said to have been abandoned because of the impurity of the water.

Salen pier used to be a regular calling point for the daily Tobermory – Oban mailboat in days gone by.

In the middle of the village a road strikes left for three miles across the isthmus to the head of Loch na Keal at Gruline. (MAPS C AND D.)

A8. DAL NA SASSUNACH

Literally, the Field of the Englishman, or stranger. About a mile beyond Salen, just before turning right across the bridge for Tobermory, there is a small field left of the road where the Mull and Morvern Agricultural Show has been held annually (apart from war years) since 1832. Few people know the old story connected with the field.

In 1609 a punitive fleet under Lord Ochiltree sailed from Ayr under orders from the Scottish Parliament to discipline the unruly Hebridean chiefs and destroy their raiding galleys. In truth, there was very good reason for this action – the Islands and Highlands had been particularly troublesome for quite some time. Anchoring in Aros Bay, off the castle (A13), Lord Ochiltree tricked the unsuspecting chiefs into meeting on board, whereupon anchors were raised and the fleet set sail. The chiefs were later released on giving an undertaking to Parliament for their good behaviour. (The Statutes of Iona).

Now, when the fleet left Aros Bay so suddenly, an English soldier was inadvertently left behind. An adaptable man, he settled to a new life, and became a shepherd to MacArthur, whose famous school of piping, second only to that of the MacCrimmons of Skye (where MacArthur had been trained), was over on the island of Ulva. (C20).

Strange to relate, the Englishman found himself to be a natural piper, with a highly retentive memory. Secretly, when far off tending the sheep, he used to practice, fingering on lengths of stick or a borrowed chanter, copying exactly MacArthur's technique, for the teacher used to practice constantly on his walking stick as he walked along with his 'tail' (servants) behind him. Anyway, one day MacArthur called together his friends and critics to hear him play a particularly difficult Pibroch (classical pipe music), *The Battle of the Birds*. To his mortification, the Englishman, thinking to give his master a pleasant surprise, chose that very day to come marching out giving a perfect rendering of the air on a set of borrowed bagpipes.

MacArthur and his sons, infuriated by the seeming insult, drew their dirks and attacked the man. Hotly pursued, he fled instinctively to the spot where he had landed, and in this field he was trapped and put to death.

A9. THE GLEN ROAD

Instead of crossing the bridge over the River Aros, continue left along the side of that fine little salmon river (fishing is private by the way) that flows out of Mull's largest loch, Loch Frisa. (A14). This is an undulating narrow moorland road up Glenaros, then down Glenbellart to Dervaig (B13, C1.) through young Forestry

plantations. The skyline is typical of Mull's plateau lava formation, with the 'steps and stairs' of successive flows now massively
eroded. (B3, D2, D8.)

A10. DRUIMTIGHMACGILLECHATTAN *(Glen Road)*

Mull's longest place name, meaning the 'Ridge of the House of
the Cattanach Man's Son'. This site lies 100 yards right of the
road at the watershed, where the road begins to turn right and
descend into Glenbellart, about 5 miles from Aros Bridge.

There is now little to see, although the low humps of old turf
tables and seats are there if the enquirer searches carefully at the
edge of the Forestry fence. Here in the old days a regular open air
barter market was held, for this was a natural centre for scattered
local communities, gone long since with only the record of ruined
houses and foundations remaining.

Thanks to the shocking state and scarcity of the Scottish coinage
before and after the Treaty of Union of 1707, barter was the ordinary medium of exchange for people whose wants were simple and
who could do without coins in their pockets (or sporrans!).

In time, this location may be covered over and lost under the
plantations of the Forestry Commission.

A11. THE BARGAIN STONE *(The Glen Road)*

Less than a mile from A10, where the road runs quite close to the
River Bellart at a road gate and cattle grid, look left across the
shallows and about 300 yards away you will see a large boulder
standing at the foot of the low escarpment down which it rolled
long since. Bargains made at the open air market were sealed
here by a shaking of hands and doubtless a sharing of drinks of
their own making. (B5, C3, C6, C14.)

A12. DESERTED VILLAGES *(Glen Road)*

About two miles short of Dervaig, beside and left of the road, there are the ruins of two little villages overlooking the boglands of Glenbellart, not far from the new hotel of Druimnacroish, which was a gaunt ruin up to a short while ago, but is now transformed into a comfortable modern holiday apartment building.

The villages are two of the more accessible reminders of the Clearances. There are others lost or forgotten on virtually every hillside and up every glen.

This road links up with routes B and C at Dervaig.

Situated 1¹/₂ miles south of Dervaig, the ruined walls of the settlement and water mill at Druimnacroish have been restored and converted into a small and friendly hotel offering excellent hospitality, comfortable accommodation, fine food and panoramic views across the Bellart Glen.

**Non-residents are also welcome for dinner –
please call to make a reservation**

Tel./Fax 01688 400274   http://www.druimnacroish.co.uk

Returning now to Aros Bridge:

A13. AROS CASTLE

This is one of Mull's three large medieval castles built in the 13th or 14th century (E10, E12).

Actually, it can be said that there are four medieval castles, for the still older fort of Dunara, near Glengorm (A19), a former stronghold of the Clan Mackinnon, who once held the north of Mull, is so extensively fortified as to merit the title of 'castle'.

Crossing the Aros river (note the span of the old bridge in passing), take the Tobermory road. After three hundred yards, at the top of the little hill, a road strikes right for half a mile to the farmhouse beside old Aros Castle.

Those massive ruined walls owed their strength more to thickness than to design. This castle was second in importance only to Ardtornish (the large square ruin on its promontory to the right of Lochaline across the Sound of Mull) as a stronghold of the Lords of the Isles in the heyday of the Highland Clan System.

The Lords of the Isles were in fact a consortium of seventeen clans under MacDonald of Islay, and for generations were a thorn in the flesh of the central Scottish Parliament: in fact, Donald Bane, one of the MacDonald chiefs, laid claim to the throne of Scotland in the 13th century. He was brother to King Malcolm III in the old Celtic line, and on the death of Malcolm he had a better claim to the throne than had Robert the Bruce, who was in the Norman line. However Bruce's Norman background was preferred to that of Donald Bane's which so infuriated him and the succeeding Lords of the Isles and Earls of Ross that they carried on a veritable vendetta for centuries with the Scottish King and Parliament.

By the way, another point not properly explained in British

(and the very rudimentary Scottish) history as taught still in our schools is the reason for the discontent and repeated revolts later by the Highland clans. The clan chiefs owed their allegiance to what they held to be the true line of Scottish kings, not to Parliament. When this line was broken and taken over by the House of Hanover the new kings were regarded as usurpers, and allegiance was still loyally given to no-one but the Stuart line, even if the last, James VI (with all his faults), had abdicated.

Aros, this particular castle of the Lords of the Isles, is defended on the seaward side by low cliffs, and originally by a ditch on the landward side. It was a strong defensive position. There is the ruin of a small chapel beside it. Built originally in the 13th century by the MacDougalls, it was possessed in turn by the Macdonalds and the Macleans.

Aros Castle

A14. LOCH FRISA

Less than a mile from A13, left of the road at the edge of the plantations, a Forestry road turns off and winds through dark tunnels of pine trees until it emerges beside Loch Frisa, the largest loch in Mull, over four miles in length. The road ends in five miles at the farmhouse of Lettermore. Boats may be hired for brown trout fishing, with the chance of a sea trout or salmon. As a result of the escape of feeding materials from the fish-farming cages into the loch, large wild brown trout are regularly caught. The indigenous trout averaged up to 3/4lb. All are beautifully spotted, red-fleshed, and fight like something twice their size. The use of less sporting spinning tackle will increase the chances of taking bigger fish, possibly a seatrout or even a salmon.

Indeed all the fishing on Mull is worth anyone's attention. The beats are never crowded – so far anyway – and the sport is usually good. These days even the ubiquitous and notorious Mull midges are not such a menace. Modern deterrents seem to have a considerable effect on them, although for myself I still prefer an old briar pipe and clouds of smoke from strong tobacco!

A15. ARDNACROSS

About five miles from Tobermory lies the farm of Ardnacross, a place of evident importance in prehistoric days. There are the ruins of a broch (*An Sean Chastail*) 600 yards north north-east of the farmhouse just above the shore line (A19, C18), and also of cairns and standing stones just over 500 yards west north-west of the house.

A mile further on, at the fourth milestone from Tobermory, is the Ghulann Dubh or Black Steep, the highest point of the road, (456 feet), with magnificent views of the whole sweep of the Sound of Mull.

A16. STANDING STONES, *Baliscate.*

Half a mile above Tom a'Mhuillin Bridge and crossroads (imme-diately above the steep descent to Tobermory), a rough road leads left for 400 yards beside Baliscate House to the Standing Stones, remains of one of Mull's many stone circles.

The large number of stone circles, standing stones, hill forts and the foundations of inexplicable buildings point to the impor-tance of Mull as an inhabited area from Megalithic times onwards.

Stone circles, Professor Thom contends, are virtually Megalithic calendars. They are designed with mathematical accuracy, pointing to specialised knowledge of surveying and astronomy. Their lay-out provided alignments on sun, moon or first magnitude stars at a fixed day of the year, thus ensuring that the date of important ceremonies, fertility rites, the solstices, etc. could be exactly foretold. (B10, B11, etc).

A17. TOBERMORY, 'TOBAR MHOIRE' *(Well of Mary)*

Scotland's Best Village (1999), with its colourful front, takes its name from the well and chapel of St Mary, for there was a small Christian settlement here from early times. The well is reputed to lie about 150 yards below the cemetery in the Upper Village. All that remains of the chapel are the foundations inside the old portion of the cemetery. A saddle quern, sometimes held to be a baptismal font, formed from a hollowed stone, was found in the ruins within recent years.

In the 1960s, following the take-over of much of the Aros

Tobermory

Estate by the Forestry Commission, the well-wooded policies surrounding the site of the demolished Drumfin House were handed over to the Tobermory people as a public park.

Near the right-hand corner, beside the boundary wall at the top of the old cemetery there is an old tombstone, cracked across and lying flat, where you can see a hole punched through the centre by a bullet fired one night towards the end of last century by grave watchers at local 'Resurrection Men' who had sneaked in to remove a body from a new grave. This took place in the last quarter of the 19th century.

Even in the islands the ghoulish trade of grave robbing was carried on, the end products being shipped in barrels of brine to the Glasgow medical school, where suitable material was hard to come by. The going rate was said to be £5 per body, a substantial sum in those days.

The author's father described how when he was a young man he joined a party of grave watchers at Pennygown cemetery for a fortnight after a burial.

There is a true story told by the author in his book *Tall Tales From An Island* describing the hair-raising trick used to identify and end the activities of the local agent and his suppliers.

Near the chapel are several old carved grave slabs of the Mackinnons of Mishnish whose lands once lay here. (A4, B8, C17, D10).

Tobermory was established in 1789 by the British Society for Encouraging Fisheries, with houses on portions of land, common grazings, and the right to cut peats, for sixty settlers, including expert fishermen from the east coast.

In spite of the advantages of a fine bay (probably the most sheltered in the Hebrides), fishing here never prospered, for Oban, on the mainland only thirty miles away, was a more natural centre. However, Tobermory became a centre for shipping, banking, and activities within the island, and even with its present population of only seven or eight hundred, it is still very much the capital of the island.

There is much to see and do in Tobermory, and there are so many places to stay, that the visitor is well advised to contact the Information Centre in Main Street. There is a host of attractions and entertainments. There are good local guide books and leaflets describing the place, and the romantic story of the Spanish galleon said to have carried a great treasure, perhaps the pay chests of the army of the Duke of Parma, which was to have invaded England, and which was blown up 300 yards off MacBrayne's pier, where the fragmented timbers lie embedded in deep hard silt under ten fathoms of water.

There are different versions of the manner in which the galleon was destroyed when about to set sail: accidentally, when powder ignited when carelessly handled during drying; by the relative of Maclean of Duart held prisoner on board, who desperately laid and fired a powder train to the magazine; by a spy of Queen Elizabeth (Tudor) named Smollett, an emissary of the English parliament (Scotland was independent and neutral then); or, in those days of practical witchcraft, by the arts of the Witch of Lochaber, who was consulted by Lady Maclean of Duart, wildly jealous of the attentions seemingly being paid by her husband to a beautiful Spanish princess on board. The witch called up an army of fairy cats, which swam out and savaged the crew to death, but one of the cats, pursuing a sailor into the magazine, set off the loose powder with the sparks from its fur.

Be all that as it may, the reader is strongly recommended to read *The Tobermory Treasure* by Alison MacLeay, which gives the true story of this glamorous wreck which was named the San Juan de Sicilia (among other names), but was *not* the *Florencia*, as popularly supposed. (C5, C11, C20, D2, D16, E11).

A18. DUN URGIBUL *(Glengorm Road)*

A visit to Glengorm is suggested, about four miles distant, with panoramic views of the whole area. Return up the steep hill beside the distillery, turn right across Tom-a'Mhuillin Bridge (The Hillock by the Mill), then sharp left, and at the crossroads 500 yards further on, take the road signposted 'Glengorm'. Just a mile beyond, opposite a gate and rough farm road, there are traces of a vitrified fort on the hillock on the skyline about 200 yards right.

This is Dun Urgibul, one of Mull's many 'Duns' or forts that lie chiefly on the west and south-west coasts, which seem to have been the easiest targets for sea raiders, even before the Vikings.

These vitrified forts are common enough in north-west Scotland and the Islands. They were built from silica-bearing rocks, with the layers of rocks embedded in branches and brush-

wood, and somehow, perhaps deliberately, or perhaps by enemy action, the wood was fired, and in the resulting great heat the rocks became vitrified, or glass-like, and fused together, so that the walls originally had great strength. (C16).

Watch out for a car park and Nature Trail through the Forestry plantations at a road bridge a mile from Glengorm, and just before that (R) the path leading to the deserted ruined settlements of Ardmore and Penalbanach, relics of the Clearances.

A19. GLENGORM *(Glengorm House)*

The policies and gardens are private, but the visitor, from vantage points on the main road, can admire the truly magnificent setting of the mansion house, with its outlook across the Sound of Mull to Ardnamurchan and the blue islands of the Hebrides. The house was built in 1860 by one James Forsyth, the new owner of Quinish and Glengorm estates during the latter days of the Clearances: five crofts and their occupants were cleared to make room for the site.

The original name for the locality was Sorne, but the name Glengorm, meaning Blue Glen, was suggested by a cynical old woman to the unsuspecting proprietor when he sought her advice on a suitable name for his fine new house. Little did he suspect that the name commemorated for all time the days when the glen was indeed blue with the smoke from the burning homesteads.

The extensive gardens of the house are now a thriving market garden, supplying much-needed produce to the area, produce which (if it was used at all), was hitherto imported from the mainland.

West of Glengorm, near the shore, are standing stones and ancient forts. Dunara is near the sea, and An Sean Dun further inland. The latter is thought to have been a broch (A15, A18). There is the deserted hamlet at Laorin, beside Loch Mingary (B13) to the west – more relics of the savage Clearances.

Formerly public roads led to Dervaig (B13) and to beyond the Mishnish Lochs (B5), now either disused or unfit for traffic; in the case of the road to Dervaig, taken over as a private Forestry road. This is a splendid walking area.

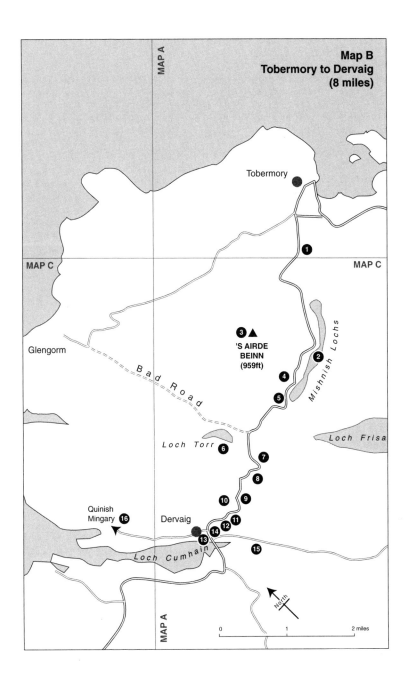

Map B
Tobermory to Dervaig
(8 miles)

MAP A

Tobermory

MAP C

MAP C

3 ▲
'S AIRDE
BEINN
(959ft)

Mishnish Lochs

Glengorm

Bad Road

Loch Frisa

Loch Torr

Quinish
Mingary **16**

Dervaig

Loch Cumhain

North

0   1   2 miles

MAP A

MAP B
Tobermory to Dervaig
(8 miles)

ONE OF THE MOST PICTURESQUE of the little roads of Mull, rising twice steeply to about 500 feet, with many horseshoe bends and blind corners. Fork left at Glengorm crossroads half a mile above Tobermory. During the popular Mull Car Rally held annually in October, which attracts up to 130 competitors, the timed section of seven miles of this road has been covered in the incredible time of seven and a half minutes. This, of course, is at night, with the road cleared of all other traffic and animals. Please do not try to match that time!

B1. MULL COMBINATION POORHOUSE

'Achafraoch House' At one and a half miles from Tobermory, left of the road and in a loop of the Tobermory burn, you see the cleared site of this building, of which only the Porter's lodge, (now a private dwelling), and a few walls remain.

Built in 1862 by a consortium of local parishes at a cost of £20,000, it was a large rambling two-storey building designed to accommodate one hundred and forty men and women rendered homeless and destitute as a result of the Clearances. Introduction of the Old Age Pension in 1909, as well as the massive reduction in population, so reduced the number of inmates that the place was no longer required. Closed down in 1925 and becoming ruinous, it was demolished in 1974. With its walled gardens, smithy, piggery, joiner's shop etc., it provided work for the inmates, preserved their will to live and was partly self-supporting.

B2. MISHNISH LOCHS

Lying left of the road for a mile and a half, ending at the fourth milestone, these are very fine fly-fishing lochs, from either boat or bank. They are in a picturesque setting, and are leased by the Tobermory Angling Club, who have placed a boat on each of the three lochs. Excellent sport is ensured by regular re-stocking. Brown trout only, often up to two or three pounds in weight. Permits from A. Brown and Son, Main Street, Tobermory.

These lochs now provide the public water supply for Tobermory, hitherto drawn from the little reservoir to the right of the road about two miles from Tobermory.

B3. 'S AIRDE BEN *(The High Hill)*

At about three and a half miles and 100 yards short of the ruined Lochs House, a wall strikes off right up the hill and continues for about a mile to the crater loch of 'S Airde Ben. Sheep tracks beside the wall offer an easy moorland walk to the summit cairn, which although at only 959 feet, gives fine views in every direction, from the blue islands north and west to Ben More and the high peaks of central Mull.

The crater loch is not very large and like all Mull lochs has its indigenous stock of brown trout, not quite up to the quality of those found in Mishnish Loch.

The hill is the eroded remnant of one of the lesser volcanic necks from which, during the Tertiary Age (50/60 million years ago), as well as from cracks in the surface of the earth, immense quantities of molten rock and ash poured out in sheet after sheet, building up what is now the island of Mull after ages of erosion. The greatest outflows came from the double volcano at the head of Loch Ba. (A9, D2, D8).

B4. BEALACH NAITHIR *(Snake Pass)*

This is the open glen at the west end of the Mishnish Lochs, so called because of its population of adders but don't be alarmed: they are timid and rarely seen, as they seek deep cover at the first hint of an approaching footfall. However, carry a stick 'in case', for it is also quite a help in hill walking, especially for the not-so-young.

B5. FUNERAL CAIRNS

Exactly at the fourth milestone at the end of the Top Loch look among the bracken at the left of the road, where you see many small cairns. In the old days, funeral parties used to pass this way to Kilmore Cemetery above Dervaig. (B12). The coffin was sometimes carried all the way on wooden bearers by relays of mourners; at other times it was on a cart.

At this spot by the roadside, the grassy bank offered a restful seat and the waters of the loch doubtless refreshed the party and diluted the bottles of whisky which used to be an integral part of each ceremony. (A11, C3, C6, C14). On leaving the spot each member of the party placed a stone until a small cairn was formed.

The name of this loch in Gaelic is 'Loch Carnan nam Amais,' which translates very accurately as the Loch of the Meeting Place. It lies exactly midway between Tobermory and Dervaig, just where the road suddenly dips steeply down towards Loch Torr (B36); a natural spot for wayfarers to rest and exchange news.

Conventional cairns are commonly seen, of course, usually at the highest point of a climb, and signify a token of achievement. At a bend half way between points B5 and B6 a very rough road strikes right for Glengorm. Not recommended for cars.

A similar track on the opposite side of the road leads to fish cages on Loch Frisa, providing an easy walk to explore the north end of the loch.

B6. LOCH TORR

At five miles Loch Torr lies at the right and below the road. This used to be the confluence of two burns that formed the Mingary Burn flowing north to an inlet in the rocky coast. In 1899 the adjoining proprietors agreed to build a damm across the narrow valley, creating this delightful loch, with its pleasant background of dark plantations.

It now carries a good stock of large rainbow and brown trout, with sea trout and the chance of a salmon in season. There are two boats on the loch. Permits to fish from the Tackle Shop, (next to Fish Farm Shop), Main Street, Tobermory.

The name comes from the symmetrical square-topped 'tor' or hillock above the road overlooking the loch.

B7. ACHNADRISH *(Field of Brambles)*

Pause beside the cairn at the summit of the steep climb above Loch Torr. Here you have one of the loveliest views in Mull towards Loch Frisa (A14), and the dominant peak of Ben Talaidh (2,496 feet) to the south-east.

B8. LEAPS OF THE GILLE REOCH

About a quarter of a mile beyond point B7, over the watershed and just short of the 6th milestone, halt at a passing place beside a boggy hollow below and left of the road. Here you will see a triangle of three little cairns 30 feet, 30 feet and 45 feet apart. They mark the site of an incident that took place in the 16th century. One day, the story goes, a MacKinnon clansman from the north of Mull (A17) was surprised by a party of Macleans over from Coll seeking to pay off old scores. This MacKinnon, who was an exceptionally agile man and an expert swordsman, was known as the Gille Reoch, or 'The Reddish Fellow' on account of the colour of his hair and complexion. Skilfully wielding his broadsword he fought off the Coll men, but, hemmed in by numbers, he took the first of his memorable leaps. Hard pressed again, he gained time by taking a second leap; but with the ring of attackers closing in for the kill he broke through by taking the most spectacular leap of all 45 feet backwards from a standing start! Measure it if you like, for the three points from which he took off are marked by the cairns. The chief of the Coll men was so exasperated by this display of agility that he hurled his claymore at the Gille Reoch, who evaded it with ease, and then, seeing his enemy disarmed, he darted in and transfixed the chief with a mighty thrust. Thoroughly deflated by the prowess of this single opponent, the attackers gave up, and carrying with them the body of their chief, they returned to their galley down at Loch Mingary.

B9. KILMORE HILL

A breathtaking view is spread out on rounding the bend at the top just above the 7th milestone. This time it is towards the west and north, with the village of Dervaig at the head of Loch Cumhain below. On clear days the hills of the Outer Hebrides can be clearly seen.

B10. KILMORE STANDING STONES

At point B9, two hundred yards right and just inside the Forestry fence, there are the remaining stones of a stone circle. An opening has been left in the fence for viewers. (A16).

B11. A CONVENIENT STONE CIRCLE

Rounding the open hairpin bend just below B9, look across the green turf of the new cemetery. Built into the boundary wall, and saving the transport of about a ton of loose stone, is one of the larger stones of yet another stone circle.

Following the Enclosures Act of the late 18th century, many such stones, as well as the stonework of old buildings, disappeared into thousands of miles of walls built during the next 100 years. It took one ton of stones to build one yard of wall 4 feet 6 inches high, so it is not surprising that the builders took what lay handy rather than carry stones from distant places. It is unfortunate that in doing so, they destroyed for ever some of the more accessible relics of a long-past age. (A16).

B12. KILMORE *('Kilcolmkill') Chapel and Cemetery*

This is a very old ecclesiastical centre, with but few traces remaining. There are some very old tombstones. Beside the entrance gate are graves of unknown sailors, victims of the wars at sea, whose bodies were found washed up in the coves and rocky beaches of the cruel western coasts.

One tombstone at the top of the cemetery has an inscribed line which is rather ambiguous at first sight. Giving the name of the deceased lady, the next line reads: *'Spouse To All'*.

However, the line below that reassures us: after 'All' the sculptor ran out of space and transferred the 'an' of 'Allan' to the next line!

B13. DERVAIG *('The Little Grove' or 'Deer Bay')*

One of the most picturesque villages in the Hebrides, built by Maclean of Coll in 1799, consisting at the time of 26 houses built in pairs, each with a large garden and grazing rights on common hill lands. The houses have now been much modernised, and are still most attractive.

There is a good hotel, and two shops, one of them the Post Office. Unfortunately, there is no petrol for sale.

Dervaig

There are some fine walks round about, especially by Loch Cumhain through Quinish estate as far as the salmon fishers' hut at Mingary – about 5 miles. The enthusiast can continue across the Mingary Burn to explore the ruined settlement of Laorin (A19), and thence to Glengorm, a long, rough walk.

There is a most interesting exhibition about Mull and its

inhabitants, animal, vegetable and human, past and present at Torr-a'Chlachain, on the outskirts of Dervaig, more fully described later (c2).

Dervaig is also a road centre for Salen (MAP A), Calgary and Torloisk (MAP C). Incidentally, the village and upper estuary were designated a Conservation Area in 1987.

B14. KILMORE PARISH CHURCH

At the crossroads beside the bridge, have a look at this little church with its attractive interior of smoothly faced stones and some good stained glass windows. Its 'pencil' steeple, of a style commonly seen in Ireland, is unusual in Scotland (c17). It was built on the site of an older church about 1905.

Coffee & Books, Dervaig

The unique island shop where you can enjoy superb coffee while you browse through our distinctive selection of books. We also offer Wines & Spirits (off-sales only), unusual cheeses, fruit & vegetables & much more...
DAILY & SUNDAY NEWSPAPERS

OPEN: Mon. to Sat. 10 to 6 (Closed 1 to 2.45)
Sunday open 1 to 3.15 p.m. (No coffee though!)
Tel: 01688 400234

B15. MULL LITTLE THEATRE

Take the left turn at the church, just short of the bridge over the River Bellart, and follow the Salen (Glen) road (A9) for less than half a mile. Above and to the left of the road lies the Mull Little Theatre, described in the Guinness Book of Records as the World's Smallest Professional Theatre.

It seats a maximum of forty three in a converted barn. It was started in 1966 by two talented young stage professionals, Marianne and Barrie Hesketh, who settled in Mull. Ambitious plays, excellently performed, attracted packed audiences. Despite the sad and untimely death of Marianne, the project has been continued and even expanded by the existing Board of Management. They audition and recruit young actors and actresses from the profession in Scotland. Still following the original principles and attracting full houses from all over the island, it is a very considerable attraction to all those who visit the island as well as when on tour on the mainland.

B16. THE QUINISH TREE

In 1984, a peculiar rock formation was discovered near Quinish

The Old Woman, part of a stone circle at Quinish standing twelve feet high.

Point by Tommy Maclean, member of an old Dervaig family. He described it to the writer of this Guide, who photographed it and reported the find to geological experts in Glasgow and Edinburgh. They identified it – subject to closer examination – as a form of fossil tree, and considered it an important discovery.

Taking the form of a solid 'pipe' of hard, brittle basaltic rock measuring 24 feet by 20 inches, it lies about 50 yards below high water mark on the rocky shore of the little bay which is blocked to the north by the low headland of Quinish Point. There are traces of similar formations nearby, but deeply embedded.

These trees are believed to have grown on the weathered surface of an early lava flow, between periods of volcanic activity,

Hebridean Whale and Dolphin Trust

Research · Education · Conservation

A **local charity**, committed to protecting whales, dolphins, and the Hebridean marine environment.

- **Find out** more in our fascinating **Visitor Centre** – displays, interactive computers, videos, and more. **Play and learn** in the "Porpoise Club" for kids.

- **Browse** in the Gift Shop, **join** the Trust or **sponsor** a whale or dolphin. **Information** on local wildlife tours and where to spot marine mammals.

- **Tell us** about sightings of whales, dolphins and porpoises in the Hebrides, and please **REPORT ANY STRANDINGS IMMEDIATELY!**

- **Open** Summer/Winter – phone for details

28 Main Street, Tobermory PA75 6NU   Tel: 01688 302620 Fax: 01688 302728
E-mail: hwdt@sol.co.uk Web site: www.gn.apc.org/whales

over 40 million years ago. The next flow overwhelmed and flattened them, but, sealed in the hot lava, the trunks were preserved by their sappy consistency. Over the years, the wood disintegrated, leaving hollow pipes which were infilled later under immense pressure by lava of a harder chemical consistency forced upwards through a network of cracks and fissures. Thus, when erosion removed the piled up lavas and beds of ash, the harder 'pipes' resisted erosion much better than the softer rocks, and isolated this stone tree trunk as we see it today.

The location is much more accessible than McCulloch's Tree (D8), and is no more than a pleasant walk through Quinish estate on the east side of Loch Cumhain, for about three miles. The track passes the 'Old Woman', the remaining twelve feet high relic of an ancient stone circle and branches to the right from the path to Mingary. Directions for the path to the tree are readily obtainable in the village.

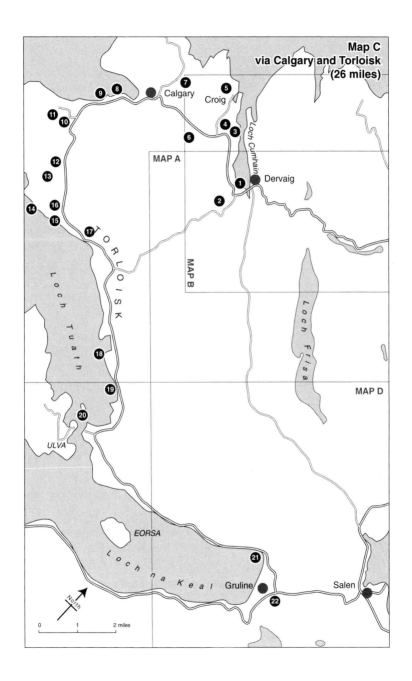

Map C
via Calgary and Torloisk
(26 miles)

Calgary
Croig
Loch Cumhain
MAP A
Dervaig
MAP B
TORLOISK
Loch Tuath
Loch Frisa
MAP D
ULVA
EORSA
Loch na Keal
Gruline
Salen
North
0 1 2 miles

MAP C
Dervaig to Gruline and Salen (at the head of Loch na Keal) via Calgary and Torloisk (26 miles)

BEYOND CALGARY THE ROAD becomes narrower and for some distance extra careful driving is advised. Some of the finest views in Mull – in fact, in the Hebrides – lie along the Torloisk section.

C1. BRIDGE OVER THE BELLART

TACKLE AND BOOKS

Main Street, Tobermory
Telephone: (01688) 302336
Fax: (01688) 302140

**Marvellous Trout
and Salmon fishing in
superb scenery**

SEA ANGLING AT ITS BEST

We stock a complete range of fishing gear from trout rods and flies to big skate traces. Tackle manufactured locally: Bridun Lures and K.F. Tackle.

*Massive selection of
local publications, maps, natural
history books, fiction and non-fiction.*

At the crossroads beside Kilmore Church, continue straight across this old bridge spanning the river Bellart which is no more than a large burn. It can have some rewarding salmon and seatrout fishing under optimum conditions. Fishing is private above the bridge, but provides a popular sport in the tidal waters of the burn mouth below. Permits can be obtained from Tackle and Books, Tobermory.

On the west side of the upper estuary you will see a

well-preserved example of a salmon trap, of which there used to be quite a number at river mouths. It consists of a level drystone dyke (open stonework) built in gentle curves from shore to shore. At high tide the wall was deeply covered and salmon drifted in seeking the invigorating waters of the burn. Often they were trapped and stranded behind the wall when the tide receded. The trap used to be maintained by successive generations of a local family. I was told by a surviving member that the record haul of stranded salmon after one high tide was sixty fish! Such bounty of the sea is almost unknown today because of commercial exploitation.

C2. HILL ROAD TO TORLOISK AND THE OLD BYRE

Half a mile beyond the bridge over the Bellart, a side road goes off left for Torloisk. Follow it for 400 yards and you will come

to the driveway leading to Torr-a'Chlachain House. Here, in the Old Byre – itself a fascinating group of buildings – there is an audio-visual display about the island of Mull. It is extremely well done, and is almost essential for the visitor as an introduction to the history, culture and natural history of the island. In addition to the audio-visual entertainment, there is an exhibition on the flora and fauna, and models of past and historical buildings. You will certainly be surprised at the wealth and variety of the flora and fauna, and of the history. Unless you are already an expert, you will certainly be enlightened. No visitor to Mull should miss The Old Byre.

After four miles this side road rejoins the coastal road near Torloisk House, ancient seat of the Macleans of Torloisk. Climbing up the steep ascent of Bealach na Sgathain 'Pass of the Mirror' (at one point a gradient of 1:3!) the road continues over moorlands, with fine views towards the islands of Ulva and Gometra and the Ben More massif of central Mull.

C3. STILL HOUSE

Two miles from Dervaig along the main Calgary road, and 200 yards short of the narrow bridge at Penmore Mill, the ruins of several cottages lie hidden among the hazel trees fifty yards right of the road beside the burn that served the mill. The left hand ruin was a 'still house', a miniature distillery, one half of which was a platform of rocks with a hemispherical hollow in the centre 5 feet by 2 feet where the fire was lit to heat the 'Black Pot' containing the mash or malted grain or its equivalent which was doubtless prepared in the other half of the house. A flue was built into the furnace to create enough draught. The 'worm' or coiled pipe from the Black Pot was cooled with water from the burn, possibly via a diverted channel condensing the vapour into raw spirit. This was the Uisge Beatha or Water of Life, or whisky. Note that the Irish equivalent is 'whiskey'.

However, this romantic history must yield to the fact that this was more probably one of the many drying kilns, whose ruined stonework is of much the same design as that of a still and 'still' house or bothy.

Whether or not that is so, certainly Mull used to produce a goodly quantity of illegal whisky in days not so long ago. (See A11, B5, C6, C14).

C4. PENMORE MILL

Just across the bridge below Point C3 lies Penmore Mill with its water wheel still in position. This was one of the many corn mills that operated in Mull up to the end of the 19th century. (D6).

In fact, every estate and large farm had its water mill. In Scotland, as in England, the miller seems to have been a very unpopular figure, and in both countries there are many folksongs about his iniquities and thievery. Anyway, he disappeared under the competition of cheaper flour from mechanised mills producing more desirable (if less nourishing) white flour, and also due, of course, to falling population in places like Mull.

C5. CROIG

One hundred yards beyond Penmore Mill a side road right leads in a mile to the inlet and tiny haven of Croig (Cro-vik, or Cattle Port). Much of the livestock of Coll, Tiree and elsewhere was landed here, driven (with the Mull cattle) by drove tracks through Mull to Grass Point (D16, E11), thence ferried to Oban to face the long drove to the markets of the south.

Croig has an atmosphere all of its own, and fine views to distant Rum and Skye.

The monument on the little island off the inlet (*Eilean na Gobha – Goat Island*) was erected in memory of the son of a former owner of Penmore estate.

Highland Cattle

An unexpected beach of white sand bites into the dark basalt cliffs half a mile to the west. The inn that once stood there is now a private house. From there came one of Mull's greatest raconteurs, Calum nan Croig, who once boasted that 'he could tie trout flies that good that spiders came down from the kitchen ceiling to take them away!'

Cruises are run from here to Staffa, the Treshnish Islands and elsewhere. (Cruises A17, C11, C20, D16, E11).

C6. DUNAULADH

Half a mile along the main road from the Croig turn-off, beside the mill burn and just where the gorge ends beside hazel bushes, the burn is crossed left by several large stepping stones called Beul an Ath, The Ford at the mouth of the Gorge. Cross them, and follow sheep tracks left for a quarter of a mile to the hillock where there are traces of an old hill fort, Dunauladh.

An old tradition says that no traveller passes Dunauladh without being offered a dram of Uisge Beatha: unfortunately,

Iron Age Fort, Torloisk

although many old traditions have been preserved in Mull, this is not one of them! (A11, B5, C3, C14).

C7. CALIACH

Nearly four miles from Dervaig, on the right, a good road branches off towards smallholdings, and ends within sight of the wild headland of Caliach, the North-west corner of Mull. It is a rough walk of a mile or so to the top of the cliffs, where winter storms have lashed the summit with blown wave tops so that little grass grows there. Caliach – the Old Woman – was so-called after a woman who, while collecting dulse (edible seaweeds), had been cut off by the rising tide but managed to climb to the top and safety. She attributed her escape not to a benevolent Providence, but to her own cleverness, for which she was punished by coming to an untimely death. A great block of stone in a cove at the headland resembles a cloaked, seated woman and that is her, doomed to sit for all eternity looking at the sea from which she escaped.

On the way to Caliach you pass Sunipol House. It used to have the reputation of being haunted by the ghosts of Australian Aborigines once hunted down and killed by bounty hunters, of whom the then occupant of this house was one. Stones were apparently thrown malevolently at the house. Actually, the stones story was correct, for they were found up to fist-size after wild storms, when they were blown by the sheer force of the wind up the clefts and chimneys of the nearby cliffs.

C8. CALGARY *(Calagharaidh)*

This is 'The Haven by the Wall', or, possibly, Cala(g)airidh, the Haven of the crofts or shielings.

Mull's loveliest, most accessible sandy bay, it is about 4 miles from Dervaig, framed by cliffs and old trees, with a wide green machair (flat grass land) above the beach. Apart from the fine mansion house and gardens in their commanding position, there are only a few houses and farms overlooking the bay, but in summer the magnificent bay is (understandably) popular. However, it seems that there is always room for everyone, even when the parking and camping areas are busy. Steps have been taken to exclude cars and campers from the machair to preserve the turf from erosion. Conveniently beside the main road an area has been set aside for a car park, camping and toilets.

There is a walk of half a mile by a cart track on the north side of the bay to Calgary Pier, now almost disused, with the remarkable geological 'dyke' or protruding wall of basaltic rock which formed a wall of the pier house. This wall may well have given Calgary its name.

East and west of the pier, on the slopes above, lie the deserted townships of Arin and Innie Vae, pathetic reminders of the evictions of the last century in the north of Mull, when emigrant ships sailed from Calgary on a one-way trip with a despairing people who, however, justified their inherited toughness and industry by laying the economic foundations of many of our former colonies.

Contrary to popular belief, Calgary, Alberta, in Canada, was not named by emigrants from Mull. In 1876, Colonel J. F. McLeod, of the North West Mounted Police, was establishing a new fort and township in Alberta. Remembering the happy days he had spent in Mull with the Laird of Calgary, he sought permission, which was gladly granted, to give the name to his new township.

C9. DRUIDS' FIELD

About three quarters of a mile beyond Calgary sands, you come to a tall scree slope and bluff on the left (Craig-a 'Chaisteal – Castle Rock), and to the right of that a short sharp dip in the road with a small flat bracken-choked space towards the edge of the cliff. This is the Druids' Field.

About 100 yards right from the foot of the dip there are two rocks with two-inch deep cup markings on their smooth western faces, while level with the ground are stones which may have been the foundations of prehistoric buildings. This was undoubtedly

Cup-marked stone near Calgary Bay

another place of pre-Christian ritual observances.

C10. HAUNN

About one and a half miles beyond Druids' Field, just short of Ensay farmhouse, a rough road goes right for half a mile to Treshnish House and gardens, residence of the late Lady Jean Rankin, for some years Lady-In-Waiting to the Queen Mother. The road continues for two miles to the old hamlet of Haunn, where some of the ruined houses have been converted to modern holiday homes.

This was for many years the home of the MacDougall families, hardy fishermen who faced the storms of this iron coast in open boats, fishing for lobsters and the harvest of the sea. They knew every inch of the cliffs and seabed, and had many tales to tell, especially about the Treshnish Islands. They kept their boats drawn up at a shallow inlet in the cliffs half a mile down a cart track from the houses. This was the location of one of the scenes in the film 'The Eye of the Needle'.

CII. TRESHNISH ISLANDS

Formed of vastly eroded piles of lava sheets, the nearest of the group lies three miles off Haunn and Treshnish Point. Landing can be difficult on those rocky shores. Even in calm weather the tide races like a river between the reefs and islets, and at other times the rollers from the open Atlantic make landing or leaving the islands a hazardous operation, so be sure the party has an experienced leader.

The islands are now uninhabited, a bird and grey seal sanctuary. A description of these islands would be a book in itself. The time to visit them is in late spring, when myriads of nesting birds and their young are a spectacle, or in late autumn, breeding time of the grey seals.

The most northerly of the islands, Cairnburg Mor (its lesser neighbour is Cairnburg Beg), with its defensive walling and embrasures for light cannon and almost vertical access path, was an impregnable fortress or prison back even in the days of the Vikings. Lunga, the largest, is fascinating to explore, with its deserted houses, cliffs packed with birds, the awesome Harp Rock (Dun Cruit), where fishermen used to span the gulf with the mast of their skiff and shin across to collect the eggs of seabirds, the cave in the centre of the island communicating with the shore to the west, and the fantastic eroded shapes of reefs and islets between the larger islands. The southernmost are Bac Mor and Bac Beag, the Large and Small Humps, the larger better known, from its shape, as the Dutchman's Hat. World famed Staffa, with its natural wonders, lies halfway towards the Isle of Ulva. (For cruises, see A17, C5, C20 D16, E11).

C12. REUDLE SCHOOLHOUSE

Look right for this tall gaunt building a mile beyond the Haunn road end, 300 yards right of the road. Once the school for children from the many scattered communities round about, it is now ruined and deserted. Scratched into the plaster of the walls you can still see graffiti of full-rigged sailing ships and the initials of scholars long gone. No rude words there, nor messages that 'Angus loves Shona'.

In front, almost hidden by heather and bracken, you can see the faint ridges of cultivation where the teacher, who lived upstairs, grew a few crops.

C13. DESERTED VILLAGES

Following the contour above C12 bear right, then left round the hill – easy moorland walking. You will see a valley opening out towards the sea, and the distant ruins among thick bracken of the villages of Crakaig and Glacgugairidh (this tongue twister means 'The Hollow of the Dark Grazings), about a mile from the schoolhouse. Examining the ruins, you will note the thickness and strength of the smoothly finished drystone walls with their rounded ends and the outside pavements of flat stones.

Certain things should be made clear about such old dwellings. The rather derogatory term 'Black House' should correctly be 'Thatched House', the confusion arising from the similarity of pronunciation of the Gaelic words for 'black' and 'thatched' (Dubh and Tughadh or Tugh). There are no chimneys in these particular houses, which means that they are pre-19th century, when chimneys were first added. Before then the peat fires were in the centre of the room, with an opening in the thatched roof for smoke to escape. Actually, peat smoke was considered to be healthy, and in any case all seats, beds, tables and other furniture were built very low, so as to be below as much of the smoke as possible.

Such houses are often referred to as insanitary hovels, but everything is relative. Outside lay the hills and fresh sea winds, with hard and heavy occupations for the people. Would you compare this with the contemporary fetid disease-ridden slums of the big cities? You will see the communal garden near the little burn that served the village, and in it an old ash tree, from whose branches a villager committed suicide by hanging many years ago. There have been well substantiated reports of the ghostly sight of an unaccountable dark figure flitting past the doorways of certain of the houses after that dark day. As many as 200 people once lived here in these houses. (A12, C14).

C14. 'STILL' CAVE

Bear right from the lower village for 200 yards towards the top of the cliff. A very rough and steep track zig-zags down to the flat raised beach at the 100 feet mark then continues straight across to descend again by a very wet and steep path at the head of a narrow cove to the boulder beach below the lower cliff. Very stiff going, but safe enough, especially coming back up the slopes, and only about half a mile in all from the village.

About 50 yards right along the top of the boulder beach there is a deeply penetrating dry cave set back in a hollow of the cliff. At the entrance is the foundation of a really large still, a platform 15 feet across, with a central hollow for the furnace 8 feet wide by 3 feet deep, with the usual flue built in below. (A11, B5, C3, C6).

Part of the platform has been covered over by rock falls from the roof. At the inner end, when the writer last visited the cave, there were still fragments of the kegs once used to hold the spirits. Every detail was well taken care of. The 'black pot' and 'worm' were probably made by the blacksmith who lived at Glacgugairidh. (C1) A turf was built along the front to hide the glow of the furnace from any infrequently passing boat; the smoke blended with the face of the cliffs. A tiny rivulet was diverted to drip across the front of the cave at the right distance to cool the worm. The whole project was invisible to the casual passer-by.

> **TREES FOR LIFE**
>
> is a Scottish charity whose aim is to regenerate and restore the native Caledonian Forest to a large area of the Highlands of Scotland and to recreate a balanced forest ecosystem.
>
> You can support us by becoming a member and/or joining us on a volunteer work week in the Highlands. For more information please contact us at:
>
> Trees for Life, The Park, Findhorn Bay, Forres IV36 3TZ.
> Tel. 01309 691292
> www.treesforlife.org.uk
>
> **Join us and help the return of the Caledonian Forest!**
>
>
> TREES FOR LIFE

The product must have been of good quality, for local fishermen and operators used to row and sail with it all the way to Ireland, where there was a good market.

Illicit distilling (there were many other centres in Mull, in fact, all over the Highlands and Islands) practically ended when in the late 1820s an Act was passed whereby the owner of the land where a still was discovered was held to be equally guilty along with the operators. Previously lairds had winked an eye at the practice, for it meant some more hard cash coming in for payment of rents.

C15. MACARTHUR'S HOUSE

Pausing at McLucas's Cairn at the summit above point C12 and admiring the view towards and across Ulva, descend the steep hill. Just before reaching the first houses left and right, you will see a substantial old ruined house and steadings on the slope 300 yards on the right. This house and land around it was gifted by a Maclean of Torloisk to a man, MacArthur, for his devoted service in bringing from Edinburgh certain valuable estate documents while closely threatened and pursued by a rival claimant to the lands.

C16. DUN AISGEAN

Continue along the brae face beyond MacArthur's House for under a mile to where the ruined Iron Age fort of Dun Aisgean can be seen on its eminence, which as usual in such forts, gives a commanding view. It is fairly well preserved, with thick walls and embrasures.

There are many such forts in Mull, mostly on the west and south-west coasts. This points to a very defensive policy in Iron Age times (from 600 BC to 400 AD.) by earlier settlers in the islands against successive waves of later and more militant invaders from Ireland before the days of the Vikings. (A18, A19, etc).

C17. KILNINIAN CHURCH

One and a half miles from C15, by steep descents and sudden bends but with rewarding views framed by wind-blasted oak trees, Kilninian Church lies left of the road. Built on the site of an earlier chapel or church, its services are conducted in collaboration with Kilmore Church, Dervaig. (B14).

There are two finely carved grave slabs in the vestry of the

church (you will find it at the back of the building). They have recently been moved there for
protection from their original position to the
right of the church door. They show a
Maclean Chief of Torloisk and his wife. Note
that such carvings are conventional, showing
the warrior in armour, with pointed helmet,
kilted garment and broadsword, perhaps
with a carved galley, or a hunting dog at
his feet. If his legs are crossed, it means
the man had taken part in the Crusades.
The woman's slab is more elaborately
carved, with shears and distaff at foot.
These are early 16th century. (A4, A17,
D10).

A few yards away is a plain tombstone to the memory of a daughter of
'Mr. Tawse, Schoolteacher', a name

Grave slab in Kilninian
churchyard

which will be illuminating to older readers who were educated in
Scotland!

C18. DUN NAN GALL

Passing Torloisk House and the junction with the hill road to
Dervaig (C2) at the east of Ballygown Bay look for the ruins of
Dun nan Gall, right, on the rocks at the edge of the shore. This
'Fort of the Strangers' is thought to have been a broch, unusual
to be found so far south in the islands. (A15, A19).

Brochs were beautifully streamlined squat 'cooling tower'
structures, each using about 10,000 tons of fitted stones to provide a defensive refuge that was impregnable for the short time
they were likely to be invested by sea raiders.

C19. EAS FORS

A mile beyond, at the little bridge among the trees, with cataracts above and below, this spectacular waterfall drops over the edge of the cliff (Dangerous! Keep Back!) into a sea pool below. It is best viewed from the shore, to which easy access is had down a grassy slope 400 yards back. 'Eas' is a Gaelic word for waterfall, while 'Fors' means exactly the same in the Scandinavian languages, showing the influence in Mull, as in many of the other islands, of the presence of the Vikings. Studies by a Norwegian researcher show that about 50% of Mull place names are of Norse extraction, and about 50% Gaelic.

C20. ULVA FERRY AND ISLE OF ULVA

Two miles beyond Eas Fors a side road branches right for Ulva Ferry, a mile distant. This is a crossing of 300 yards or so, held to be the scene of Thomas Campbell's poem Lord Ullin's Daughter, written when he was tutor at Sunipol, near Calgary. (C7) Local people consider a ring of boulders above high water mark a few hundred yards east to be the grave where the girl's body was buried after being found washed up. It is more likely that the correct scene of the tragedy was the longer crossing from Gribun (D5) to the south shore of Ulva, which was formerly one of the lines of communication before the days of passable roads. This is across Loch na Keal, a stormy exposed sea loch under certain conditions.

Thomas Campbell (later to become Poet Laureate, although certainly one of the most forgettable ones), with his indifferent memory, may have referred to the loch as Lochgyle. The whole poem is surely a flight of fancy based on a local tradition.

Few people have heard of the romantic connections between the great missionary explorer Dr Livingstone and Mull and Ulva. The Livingstones were descended from the famous Beatons, Doctors of Pennyghael (D12), named the Royal Physicians of the Isles. Dr Livingstone's grandfather was a highly respected crofter in Ulva before he moved with his family to Blantyre, where in due course his grandson, David, was born in 1813.

Now, this Niall Mor was one of the two Livingstone brothers who one night defied the law by cutting down and reverently interring in an island in Loch Linnhe what was left of the body of James Stewart – James of the Glen – which had been hung in chains for three years at Ballachulish Ferry on a gibbet always under guard.

It is a minor but still grim incident in Scottish clan history that James Stewart, a respectable farmer, was condemned and executed for a crime he certainly did not commit 'by a Campbell judge before a Campbell jury', simply because the Campbells were at enmity with the Clan Stewart. You will read about it in Stevenson's *Kidnapped* and *Catriona*.

Fearing retribution, the two brothers left the district and finally settled in Ulva.

Part of the house where Dr Johnson and Boswell were entertained by the old Chief of Ulva can still be seen in the Structure of the Factor's house.

In the 1840s, Ulva became the scene of some of the most callous and unnecessary Clearances in the Hebrides. The population

Fingal's Cave

in 1840 was 800, according to the Statistical Account. By 1850 it had fallen to 200. The island ultimately became a bracken-infested waste dotted with ruined houses. The late owner, Lady Congleton, and her nephew Lt. Col. Howard, the owner of adjoining Gometra, have revived much of the natural resources with valuable herds of pedigree cattle and flocks of sheep, providing work for a small but increasing staff. Since taking over the estate, Col. Howard has opened up the island to the public, with its diverse attractions. However, the many ruined houses and settlements keep reminding the visitor of the days of cruelty and oppression of the 19th century.

Once on the island, keeping left along estate roads and paths skirting the policies of Ulva House, and passing below the unique burial place of three generations of lairds on the summit of the old fortress hill Dun Bheoramuill, the visitor will arrive after one and a half miles at the stretch of columnar basalts along the shore line called 'The Castles'. According to Banks, the geologist, the formations here rival their better-known counterparts in Staffa. At Ulva Ferry, information can be had on cruises based on the jetty there. (A17, C5, CLL, D16, E11).

C21. RIVER BA

Killiechronan House

Situated at the head of Loch na Keal on its own Estate running five miles down the North side of Loch na Kea. A four-star, country house hotel with elegant furnishings emulating the wonderful meals prepared mainly with local fresh ingredients and for which the AA has awarded a rosette.

Open from March to October Non residents welcome for Dinner every evening and, **Traditional Sunday Lunch**. Accommodation is limited; please be sure to make a reservation to avoid disappointment.

reservations & information
tel. 01680 300403 - fax. 01680 300463

The final six miles of Route C give some of the best views in Mull through woods of natural oak across Loch na Keal to Ben More and the cliffs of Gribun. The River Ba, flowing out of Loch Ba (Loch of the Cattle) is probably the finest salmon river in Mull. Permits to fish may be had from the estate office of Killiechronan (Singing Woods) beside the river mouth. Loch na Keal (Loch of the Cells of Missionaries) was an important naval anchorage in both World Wars.

C22.

Arrive at the road junction near Gruline where a short road cuts across the isthmus for three miles to Salen (A7). However, take the road right for Gruline and Route D.

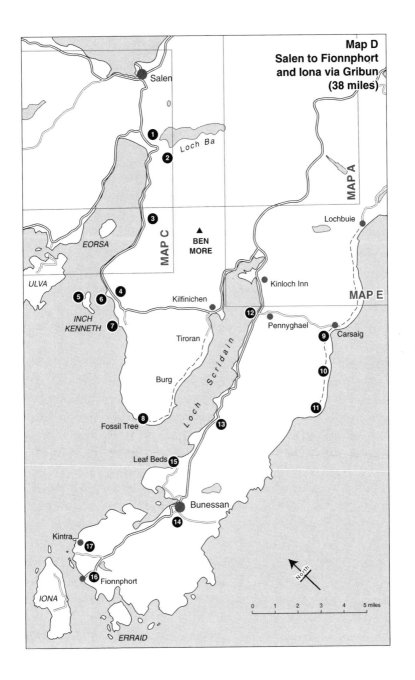

Map D
Salen to Fionnphort
and Iona via Gribun
(38 miles)

Salen to Fionnphort and Iona
via Gribun
(38 miles)

D1. MAUSOLEUM OF MAJOR-GENERAL LACHLAN MACQUARIE

A signpost half a mile past the crossroads at C22 points left to the mausoleum, which lies a quarter of a mile along the rhodo-dendron-lined drive to Gruline House. Born in 1761 of Ulva farming folk, he joined the army and rose all the way through the ranks to be Major-General and Governor-General of New South Wales between 1809 and 1820.

His energy and initiative opened up the whole of the eastern Australian seaboard, where many of the names are from his family and from Mull. General Macquarie was well worthy of greater recognition, but unfortunately he had influential political enemies both in Australia and London, who were jealous of his success, who belittled his achievements and opposed his advancement. He brought a new humanity into the convict settlements, aided by his wife. In fact, it is reported that there were minor crimes committed in Britain, during Macquarie's time as Governor-General, by despairing and desperate people, who hoped that they would be transported to a new and better life as a convict in New South Wales.

He bought the estate between Loch na Keal and Salen, which he called Jarvisfield, and founded the village of Salen in 1808. (A7) His achievements are recorded on the marble slabs at the ends of the little building, and justify the name by which he is still remembered: 'Father of Australia.' Until recent years the mausoleum was maintained by the Government of New South Wales, but has now been taken over by the Ministry of Works.

D2. LOCH BA ('Loch of the Cattle')

Half a mile after D1, immediately across the narrow bridge spanning the River Ba at Knock Farm, note the signpost pointing left to the Rights of Way along the shore of Loch Ba that climb by hill passes south to Kinloch Inn and Glenmore. (E3).

This is the centre of sporting estates, with mansion houses at Gruline and Knock, and a shooting lodge beside a lovely tree-fringed bay on Loch Ba. It would be wise, perhaps, to check at the farm before going on the hill during the stalking season.

Permission may be had to take a car half a mile along the private road to the loch, which may be fished on application to Killiechronan Estate Office. (C21) It is the second largest loch in Mull, almost three miles in length.

Ben Chasgidle (1,632 feet) is one of the eroded cores of the five-mile diameter double volcano that existed here during the Tertiary Age, fifty to sixty million years ago, reaching an estimated height of 8 to 9,000 feet. From it came most of the lava flows that covered the ancient land floor, now much eroded and reclaimed by the sea. (A9, B3, B16, D8) It is a wonderful centre for geologists.

The Right of Way follows the west side of the loch for one and a half miles (E5), ascends Glen Clachaig, crosses a spur of Ben More and descends to Kinloch, an eight mile walk for the energetic. This was once a twice-weekly walk for the postman from Salen, who met his colleague from the Ross of Mull and then continued to Grass Point with and for the mail. (E11).

Another Right Of Way, used regularly for hundreds of years, forks left at the mouth of Glen Clachaig, and, continuing to the head of the loch and up Glen Cannel, with its ruined settlement, crosses hill passes to descend to Glen More.

There is one very sad story connected with Loch Ba. Once upon a time the waters of the loch had the magical quality of restoring youth to the aged. This was in the days of the giantess the Caliach Bheur, the witch of Mull, who lived so long ago that her herds of deer used to graze on lands far to the west of Mull now reclaimed by the sea. She was so tall that she could wade across the Sound of Mull no more than knee deep, and the smaller islands were formed from the earth and stones spilt from a creel she once carried.

Now this Caliach grew old like everyone else, but she had the special power of restoring her girlhood again and again by immersing herself in the waters of Loch Ba early on the morning of each 100th birthday, provided that she did so before any living creature had uttered its first call of the day within her hearing. Alas, as the aged giantess tottered down to the pebbly shore on her last 100th birthday, to her despair she heard the distant bark of a restless collie dog. The spell was broken, and the Caliach expired just yards from the waters of eternal youth.

I have always been sorry for the fate of this benevolent witch, for I have heard of no malpractices on her part. She even refused to cast a spell to sink the Spanish Galleon in Tobermory Bay at the behest of the jealous wife of the Chief of Duart – that was finally the work of the Great Witch of Lochaber, but that is another story. (A17).

D3. ASCENT OF BEN MORE *(3,169 feet)*

This is the highest mountain of tertiary basalts in Britain: a 'Munro' that attracts many 'Munro-baggers' to Mull to add another in their ambition to cover all 284 Munros in Scotland.

What we recommend is based on the Bartholomew 1/2 inch

map of Mull. We have mentioned the shortest and easiest line to the top, starting at D3, following the burn and crossing over. Information can be confirmed at the farms. I prefer the climb from the north or east of the Ben (by Ben Fhada) which presents a constantly increasing view. Two items of advice: this is one of the best stalking areas in Mull. After mid-season it is both safe and courteous to check at Gruline or at Torosay Castle that there are no stalking arrangements. Secondly even on the finest summer day, carry a light pullover to wear at the summit of the Ben. Temperatures can be 10 degrees F lower than down beside Loch na Keal.

D4. GRIBUN AND 'TRAGEDY ROCK'

Three miles beyond Dishaig the traveller turns suddenly into a grim shadowed world of rocks where the road winds under crumbling 1,000 foot cliffs with a drop of 50 feet to the shore below. After half a mile of this the cliffs recede and there are a few scattered houses. Between the road and shore there are outcrops of hard grey sandstone containing masses of fossils, chiefly small mussel shells (Arcuata Gryphaea), commonly called 'Devil's Toenails', laid down in an ancient sea around 100 million years ago. (D9) This is Gribun.

In about a mile, when you come to a farmhouse on the right beside the road in a clump of windblown trees, look directly opposite on the left, and forty yards from the road you will see an enormous boulder with a low wall against it. In the late 18th century a tiny cot house stood there, which had just been let to a shepherd from the Ross of Mull and his local wife-to-be. The day of the wedding was wild and stormy, with heavy rain, but all went well with the ceremony. Late in the evening the young couple slipped away from the celebrations in the barn on the other side of the road, and retired to this little house. They were never seen again. Above them in the night a gigantic boulder split in two, one half rolling down for fifty yards and crushing the house and its occupants into the ground. A few flowers still grow beside the little wall.

D5. INCH KENNETH

The shorter access road to the landing slip at the ferry strikes right soon after D4, but the ferry is private. A short distance from the slip to the east there is a beach of dark basaltic sand, from where the ferry boats to Ulva leave. (C20).

Second in sanctity to Iona, Inch Kenneth is a fertile little island called after Kenneth, a disciple of St Columba. There is a modern farmhouse and a three-storey mansion house to which some notoriety attaches through its associations with the Mitford family.

In 1937, Lord Redesdale purchased the island from Sir Harold Boulton. The Redesdales, or Mitfords, were a remarkable family, with remarkable girl children, most of whom made a clear mark on life. There were close relations before World War Two between some of the Mitfords and the British Union of Fascists, under Sir Oswald Mosley, who, in fact, married Diana, one of the daughters. However, it was a younger daughter, Unity, who attained the widest notoriety through her unbounded admiration for Hitler and his ambitions. He in turn seemed to be charmed to have the attention of this glamorous young lady, and perhaps hoped to exert some influence in Britain through the association.

However, when war between Britain and Germany became imminent she attempted to commit suicide with a small pistol she always carried, and which had been given her by Hitler. In this, as in everything else, she failed, but the head wound she inflicted on herself left her a semi-invalid, or worse, and she was shipped home from Germany, and died on the island in 1948.

Another daughter, Jessica, who was, and is, a communist, became the finest writer in a family of fine writers, and recorded their strange childhood in that strange family in a remarkable book, still well worth reading, called *Hons. and Rebels*. She records that most of the windows in their various homes were decorated somewhere with a swastika diamond-scratched on the glass by one of the daughters, and that each one was surmounted by a carefully executed hammer and sickle, which she had done.

There is a ruined pre-reformation chapel surrounded by many old grave slabs, and just beside the chapel the elaborately carved tombstone of Sir Alan Maclean of Knock. There are still traces of the old house where Dr Johnson and Boswell were so hospitably entertained. (C20). The island is closed to the public.

D6. MILLSTONES

Just one hundred yards left (west) of the ferry slipway, on the Mull side, at the end of an old fence above the shore, there lies a millstone partly cut out of the bed of hard grey sandstone, which, in the days of milling, provided 20 or 30 high quality millstones per year. There was quite an industry of extracting, shaping and exporting them from the shore here.

D7. MACENNON'S CAVE

About half a mile beyond the side road to the ferry a farmtrack forks right to Balmeanach Farm, an oasis of arable land surrounded by an amphitheatre of tall cliffs.

Leave the car at the farm and take the path to the cave which is roughly signposted. After about three quarters of a mile a gate in the fence at the edge of the cliff (wonderful cliff scenery here) leads to a very steep path, involving some scrambling and wet mud, but which descends to the boulder beach. A very rough scramble across the boulders for two hundred yards brings one to the mouth of the cave which is the most deeply penetrating in Mull.

Be sure to arrive at half tide on a falling tide, as the mouth of the cave is tidal. It lies beside a feathery little waterfall which probably supplied the needs of the Abbot MacKinnon, after whom the cave is named. His tomb lies beside the altar in Iona Cathedral. Dr Johnson was awed, and not without reason, by the huge proportions of the entrance to this cave, which penetrates for hundreds of yards into total darkness.

It opens out into a wide chamber where lies a square block of rock called 'Fingal's Table', or, perhaps, 'Maclean's Table', beyond which the cave is blocked by rockfalls. Torches or candles are essential, if only to keep at bay the malevolent fairies of the cave who once killed every member of an exploring party led by a piper. Him they spared because of his music, until he had to give up playing through sheer exhaustion. Then they killed him. It is true that this happened some time ago! I always feel strongly uneasy here, and hope my light will not go out!

D8. MCCULLOCH'S FOSSIL TREE, *Burg*

The objective here is the cast of the fossilised section of a 40ft pine tree exposed in the lower cliff, just above high water mark, in the headland of Ardmeanach (or Burg), in a National Trust property known as The Wilderness – a wilderness of rocks and cliffs. It was discovered in 1819 by the famous geologist McCulloch. The road climbs up from Gribun and runs down Glen Siolisdair (Iris Glen) for four miles to Kilfinichen Church on the shore of Loch Scridain. Here a road diverges R along the shore for a mile, where it passes above the sun-trap of Tiroran House, now a private hotel.

Just beyond, at the end of the wood where a small stream

flows across the road, is as far as a car should be driven, for beyond this the road becomes very rough indeed. In any case, it is a pleasant walk for the next four miles past the farm house of Tavool to the last outpost, Burg farmhouse. There are now two further miles of hard, but safe going past the Iron Age fort of Dun Bhuirg and beside it the lonely memorial erected to the memory of Daisy Cheape, a daughter of the late General Cheape, a former owner of Tiroran, who was drowned in Loch Scridain below and is interred at Carsaig (D9). Then as the 1,000ft cliffs begin to tower above, follow the narrow sheep and wild goat tracks along the steep grassy slope at the foot of the cliffs. There are two approaches to the Tree. After about a mile, where strange, wheel-like formations appear on the shore below (can they be isolated tree-trunks eroded level with the rocks?), descend by a grassy glissade, climb down 10ft of 'steps' on a worn outcrop of columnar basalt, and proceed by rough going, rewarded by the fascinating rock formations, along the boulder beach to a point 100yds beyond the second (northern) branch of the small double waterfall that drops down the face of the cliff. This approach is tidal, so to ensure access to the tree at all times, continue along the path above the lower cliff in which the Tree stands to where a ladder of iron rungs, quite safe to use with ordinary care, is set into the face of the cliff beside the Tree.

This tree must have been one of a number growing on the pre-tertiary land surface when it was overwhelmed – drowned – by the first great lava flow from Ben More (A9, B3, D2) about 60 million years ago, yet its bulk retained just enough cooling influence to preserve its shape in the solidifying lava, which has been massively eroded away to exhibit this cross-section, a 3ft high, 5ft diameter of the lower trunk. On the surface you can see fibres of the original wood silicified into stone. In a deep recess there is still some of the original charcoal from the scorched wood as fresh as when it was charred by the engulfing lava. Please do not attempt to touch it, as it is irreplaceable and is one of the natural wonders of Britain. Around the site more traces of fossilised wood are embedded in the columnar basalts of fantastic shapes and colours – in fact, this is a little-known area of columnar basalts which if more accessible would rival the formations on Staffa and Ulva (C 720). A marvellous place for the energetic to explore.

D9. CARSAIG

Continue from Kilfinichen towards Kinloch, at the head of Loch Scridain, noting along the shore the flat slabs of rock deeply scored by stones embedded in the ice of the Glen More glacier as it moved westwards during the Ice Age.

Keep right at the junction with the new road through Glen More. (MAP E). In two miles, crossing the bridge at the hamlet of Pennyghael, you come to a road sign pointing left up the hill to Carsaig. Four miles from here, the narrow moorland road reaches the end of an escarpment and drops very steeply through tall trees to end at the old pier, which stands at the east end of Carsaig Bay, with its beach of dark sand. Above it lies a sloping area of grassland, the whole lying within a semi-circle of 700 ft. cliffs, down which streams fall like white veils. It is one of the most dramatic scenes in Mull. The field above the shore slopes up to a small walled cemetery where General Cheape's daughter was buried. (D8).

Now, a word of warning and a very urgent request. It is most inadvisable to take a car beyond where the moorland road ends at the top. It is best to park there and walk down, and in return for access, visitors should keep to the shore and avoid the precincts of Inniemore Lodge, where there is the Summer School of Painting (and where more inspiring?).

From the pier a right-of-way follows the shoreline eastwards for about four miles to Lochbuie (E10). But continue westwards along the shore towards the bold headland on the west side; then by rough but level going for a mile below the cliffs and you come to the Nuns' Cave and tidal quarry. The high cliffs extend in an unbroken line, composed of sandstone layers overlain by columnar basalts. The formations are fantastic, and the lower sandstones are highly fossiliferous (D4).

D10. NUN'S CAVE AND SANDSTONE QUARRY

Just short of a fine waterfall, where an exceptionally steep grassy slope gives access to the cliff top (The Nun's Pass), this cave lies 50 yards from the shore above the raised beach.

In front lies a horizontal tidal quarry of hard grey sandstone which was much used by the monks of Iona as a material for carvings. Wooden wedges were driven into cracks in the rocks, and those wedges expanded when covered by the tides, and forced the slabs apart. They were then carried up to the Nun's Cave and carved into ornamentation for Iona Cathedral, and also into grave slabs etc., which were sold to augment the funds of the Church.

The floor of the cave is deeply littered with stone chippings under the modern detritus. On the left hand, or west, wall of the cave are carved holy symbols, crosses, etc., the work of the stone-carving monks in idle moments. A font is chiselled into the rock at the mouth of the cave. The place is called after the Nuns who were evicted from Iona at the Reformation and sheltered here for a time. (A4, A17, C17).

D11. CARSAIG ARCHES

An energetic explorer can continue for a further two miles west along very rough going just above the rocky shore to the Carsaig Arches, where the columnar bassalts have been eroded into caves, arches and strange shapes. Be careful and watch your footholds when inspecting the area.

Above the Carsaig Arches, accessible from the landward side, thin seams of poor quality coal (lignite) are found on the lower slopes of Ben an Aoinaidh. The Gaelic name of one stream is Allt nan Ghual, translated as 'Burn of Coal', where a seam thick enough to work has been cut through and exposed.

A measure of coal once figured as part of the rent paid by the farm of Shiaba which is two miles distant; and for a time coal was carted along a rough moorland track for use in the smithy at Pennyghael. Research and testing in recent years confirmed that the coal was too poor in quality and the seams too thin and inaccessible for commercial exploitation.

It is a remote area, and reference to the Ordnance Survey map would be helpful. Probably the best approach is from near Beach Farm (pronounced 'Bee-ach') that lies off the main road about four miles west of Pennyghael. A very old track crosses the moors, arriving in four miles at the ruins of Airidh mhic Cribhain, just south of which the coal seams can be found on the lower slopes of the valley on both sides. 'Coal Burn' lies higher up on the east side. Other approaches are long and dangerous. Although the author has never used this approach to the Carsaig Arches, it might be quite feasible, for there is access to the shore below.

D12. BEATON CAIRN

Returning to the main road at Pennyghael, continue for half a mile beyond the Free Church (right), then eighty yards from the road on the right a simple cairn will be seen above the shore, surmounted by a cross, half hidden now by low bushes. This cairn was raised many years ago in memory of the Beatons, the famous 'Ollamnh Muileach' or Mull doctors, who came originally from Bethune, in France, and who were skilled in the use of herbs.

They were physicians first to the Lords of the Isles, and later to the Macleans of Duart. Their fame even reached the ears of King James VI, who, after convening the greatest doctors in the land, set them a test to find the most skilled of all. This honour fell to the Mull Beaton, who received a grant of land. Unfortunately, he was poisoned by jealous colleagues, who first took the precaution of removing every antidote Beaton could call for. The shaft of the cross bears the much eroded markings: G M B 1582 D M B, the initials of two of the most famous Beatons.

Cairn and cross at Pennyghael commemorating the Beatons

A few miles further on you will pass a walled enclosure said to have been the place where the Beatons grew the herbs used in their treatments.

D13. MARY MACDONALD CAIRN

Nearing the village of Bunessan, above and to the left of a straight section of good road, there stands a square memorial cairn to Mary MacDonald, a humble countrywoman who lived in the district. She was born in 1817, and died in 1872. She had,

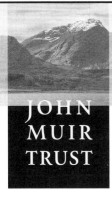

JOHN MUIR TRUST

Protecting Scottish Wild Places

For further information contact the Trust Director Nigel Hawkins at John Muir Trust 41 Commercial Street Leith, Edinburgh, EH6 6JD

Tel: 0131 554 0114 www.jmt.org

The John Muir Trust is guardian of some of the finest wild landscape in the Scottish Highlands and Islands.

Dedicated to working with local communities in the conservation of these wonderful areas, the Trust looks after all the many things that make up wild places - the birds, animals, plants, insects, rocks, lochs, rivers, coastlines - and the interest of visitors.

The Trust owns two of Scotland's finest mountains - Bla Bheinn in the Black Cuillin of Skye and Ladhar Bheinn in the wild bounds of Knoydart. The Trust's lands extend right into Loch Coruisk in the heart of Skye's Black Cuillin. The remote and extremely beautiful Sandwood Estate in Sutherland is also in the guardianship of the Trust.

If you would like to help please consider becoming a member of the JOHN MUIR TRUST and by doing so play your part in helping to protect and cherish our wonderful heritage of wild places.

of course, no knowledge of written or spoken English and in her native Gaelic she composed that most beautiful hymn Leanabh an Aigh, (Child in the Manger), translated into English by Lachlan MacBean, who died in 1931. The tune to which the words are set is an old Gaelic air that was given the name 'Bunessan' (all hymns have an identifying name) by the person who adapted it. In a modern setting, it has received the rather doubtful honour of inclusion in the Hit Parade.

D14. BUNESSAN

This trim village is central to the crofting area of Mull, a flatter area of different geological composition. With its shops, hotel, Post Office, pier, etc., it is an excellent centre for exploring the little crofting hamlets, the old chapel of Kilviceon, the Fossil Leaf Beds of Artun, angling in the local lochs, and so on. It lies five miles from the road terminus at Fionnphort, and at the side of Loch na Lathaich, a good anchorage for small craft.

D14A.

A mile or so beyond Bunessan, a track to the right takes one to a building at the edge of the sea abandoned by salmon fishermen. In the early days of the Iona Community an upstairs room, where nets had been stored, was used as a little chapel, where some baptisms were held; it became known as the Chapel of the Nets.

D15. FOSSIL LEAF BED, *Ardtun*

Just before entering the village of Bunessan, take the side road (right) along the shore past scattered houses for about a mile. Proceed on foot across the level moorland towards a little square-shaped hillock on the skyline, then strike diagonally left to the edge of the cliff – an easy walk of about a mile. Here there

are extensive areas of columnar basalts on the shore and the lower cliffs, and in a cove biting into the cliff there are several layers of dark mudstone sandwiched between the basalts. These layers were deposited at different periods, evidence of how detritus, mud, and growing things gathered in still lake waters during long periods between lava flows. Access can be precarious.

In certain of the layers are found leaves and flowers beautifully preserved where they sank through quiet waters under subtropical conditions, and gathered on the bottom, where eventually they were covered by other detritus slowly drifting down, and then by vast heavy flows of lava, which converted their transient softness into lovely stone fossils. They were first reported by the then Duke of Argyll in 1851.

D16. FIONNPHORT

The tiny port with the white sands, pink granite and translucent water beloved by painters. From here, where the road ends, a regular ferry crosses the mile-wide Sound of Iona to the Sacred Island.

Like Bunessan, side roads lead to little crofting communities. Erraid, the tidal island so important in David Balfour's adventures in Mull, depicted in *Kidnapped*, lies one a half miles south, a district well known to Robert Louis Stevenson, where his uncle had his headquarters during the building of Dubh-hirteach (which means, perhaps, The Black Deadly Place, and is well named) and Skerryvore Lighthouses. The author's lesser-known story *The Merry Men* also centres here.

Two miles north is the little harbour of Kintra, another cattle importing centre in former days. (C5, E11) Fionnphort is another centre for local cruises. (A17, C5, C20, C11, E11).

Less than two miles south of Fionnphort lies the little centre of Tireragan, where on land donated for the purpose, where there were once five settlements and scattered houses now ruins, a new township is to be developed as a showpiece, the houses to have all modern facilities, yet to blend with the landscape, and restore something of the former methods of agriculture and stock-raising.

Tireragan Rural Development Project on the Ross of Mull

Highland Renewal, a Scottish Charity, is developing a remote rural area on the *Ross of Mull*, once the home of more than 150 people who were cleared for sheep farming. An old clachan is being restored, woods are being planted, a 7km deer fence keeps out stock on this beautiful 625ha. land. A market garden and tree nursery are being established. Over 10 km of footpaths, including a nature trail, are open to the public. Come and walk or take part in the project as a volunteer. Education involving local schools and university research is a major focus of the project.

Further information is available on our Web site: **http://ourworld.compuserve.com/homepages/highlandren**

Or contact Highland Renewal, Taigh Sithe, Knockvologan, Fionnphort, Isle of Mull, PA66 6BN.

Telephone: 01681 700587. Email highlandren@compuserve.com

D17. TORMORE GRANITE QUARRIES

An easy walk of half a mile north of Fionnphort. Quarrying of the lovely red or pink granite of the Ross of Mull was an important industry until the start of World War I. You can read details in Joan Faithfull's book 'The Ross of Mull Granite Quarries' published by the New Iona Press. Dozens of large squared rectangular blocks lay abandoned on the site until the early 1980s, when the firm of Stewart McGlashan Ltd. (later Scottish Natural Stones Ltd.), received permission to re-open the quarry. The blocks were conveyed to the Company's Works at Shotts, and later for final dressing to Aberdeen. This specialised work did not create much local employment, and no stone has been removed since 1997.

The site is well worth a visit. It lies above a picturesque little sandy bay, where a steep tramway ran down to a pier conveying the granite for shipment. For years it was exported all over the world: at home, for the building of Blackfriars Bridge and Holborn Viaduct and part of the Albert Memorial in London, the Liverpool Docks, Jamica Bridge in Glasgow. Handsome red curling stones were produced until replaced by the harder, darker granites of Ailsa Craig and Wales. (Half a dozen of those red stones lie at the bottom of the Mishnish Loch Pellac, where they fell through the ice just before World War I!)

The little bay, known as the Bullhole, a sheltered anchorage for yachtmen, is protected by Eilean nam Ban (Womens' Island) to which St Columba is said to have banished all women from Iona!

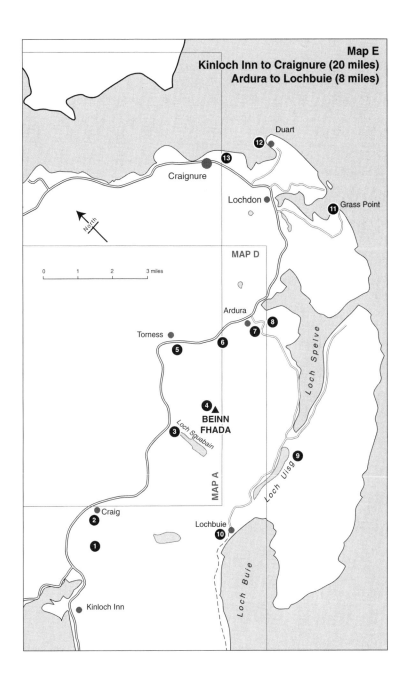

Map E
Kinloch Inn to Craignure (20 miles)
Ardura to Lochbuie (8 miles)

Duart

Craignure

Lochdon

Grass Point

MAP D

North

0   1   2   3 miles

Ardura

Torness

Loch Spelve

BEINN
FHADA

Loch Sguabain

Loch Uisg

MAP A

Craig

Lochbuie

Loch Uisg

Kinloch Inn

Loch Buie

95

Kinloch Inn to Craignure, by Glenmore (20 miles)

RETURN TO KINLOCH INN, at the head of Loch Scridain, then:

E1. DERRY NA CULEN

Half a mile from Kinloch, following the main road right through Glen More, at the end of the right of way from Loch Ba (D2), just at an old sheep fank, a track leads right to the River Coladoir, which it skirts for a mile to the ruins of Derry na Culen, a typical old two-storey farmhouse, with outbuildings and a large sheep fank (fold or enclosure), backed by a steep hill slope down which a little stream drops in a 50 foot waterfall.

This old farmhouse in its picturesque setting is worth a visit. Along the course of the river are seen huge boulders carried and deposited by the retreating glacier that once flowed down Glen More, and bare stretches of ice-grooved rocks.

E2. CRAIG

About a mile further on, on the flat boggy land beyond the shepherd's disused cottage of Craig (now modernised) and beside Loch Sguabain (E3), a bitter clan fight took place between the Chief of the MacLaines of Lochbuie (assisted by his brother, Maclean of Duart) and his son Ewen – Ewen a'Chinn Bhig, or Ewen of the Little Head.

Nagged to distraction by a greedy wife, Ewen pestered his father for more and more land until finally his father flatly refused any further concession. Supporters of both factions met here, and in the course of a bitter fight, probably near Ceann a'Chnocain, the highest point of the new road, Ewen was decapitated by the sweep of an adversary's broadsword, thus fulfilling the prophesy of death foretold the day before by a fairy woman. Jammed in the stirrups, the headless corpse was carried by the maddened horse for nearly four miles, until, facing the steep climb after fording the river Lussa above the falls, the animal halted, exhausted, and the corpse fell to the ground. The exact spot is still marked by a tiny overgrown cairn. (E5).

E3. LOCH AND CLACH SGUABAIN

Glen More, the Big Glen, is a typically narrow glaciated valley, with ice-scored rocks, moraine mounds and hill slopes smoothly planed down by the glacier that flowed to the west here up to 10,000 years ago. Hill paths lead across the ridges to Loch Ba (D2).

Gloomy and windswept, it is the most romantic glen in Mull, a focal point for traditions and folklore. For instance, nine miles from Kinloch, you see below you three lochs, Loch Sguabain being the nearest. Near its outflow lies the island stronghold of Ewen of the Little Head (E2). From it the River Lussa flows down to Loch Spelve, a fine little salmon river (fishing permits from Torosay Castle and from Tackle and Books, Tobermory). (E13).

Above this point, one hundred yards below the new road, a huge pointed boulder stands at a lay-by on the old road. This is known as Clach Sguabain, or Sguabain's Stone. The story goes that Sguabain, one of the legendary giants of Fingal, was standing here one day, minding his own business. Nicol, another of the giants, standing a few miles away beside Loch Spelve, started a heated argument across the intervening hills. Losing his temper, he bent down and tore out a boulder which he tossed pettishly over at Sguabain. He, not to be outdone, unearthed an equally large missile and heaved it back at Nicol. Their aim was probably poor, for there is no record of personal injuries: but as evidence of the fracas, Nicol's stone, confusingly called Clach Sguabain, still stands there beside the road, while Sguabain's stone can be seen on the shore of Loch Spelve where Nicol stood.

E4. THE DRAGON OF GLENMORE

East of Loch Sguabain stands Beinn Fhada (1,603 feet), The Long Hill, on the top of which was the lair of a dragon that terrorised the glen. A long hollow can still be seen here, worn into the shape of its scaly body.

Anyway, so fierce a dragon was this that the local king (there were many little kings in those days) offered a portion of his lands and the hand of his daughter to anyone who would rid him of this importunate beast. Knights and adventurers all had a go, but they all vanished into the fiery maw of the dragon.

Then one day a quiet young man landed from a galley just off the Kinloch. First of all he laid down a floating causeway of barrels, into which he drove projecting spikes, between ship and shore. Then, armed with no more than his sgian dubh or black knife he landed a herd of cattle and began to drive them up the glen towards the dragon's lair. (This Sgian Dubh, incidentally, is the very same black knife that the kilted Highlander of today still carries in his right stocking – the Black Knife of Mercy that ends the life of any wounded adversary.)

Seeing this, down leaped the incredulous beast to enjoy his feast, doubtless thinking to himself 'They'll never learn!' But it was to be different this time. Quickly turning the herd, the young man slaughtered one of them as soon as the dragon's breath became hot on their backs. Halting to devour the cattle beast, the dragon lost ground, but soon overhauled his prey again, and so another beast was slaughtered, with the same result. As fast as the dragon came up it was halted by the sacrifice of another of the herd, until only one old cow was left, but this was at the landward end of the causeway. Leaping nimbly between the spikes, the young man went on board his galley, but when the greedy dragon tried to follow him, it became hopelessly impaled on the spikes and was easily dispatched.

The dead dragon was duly towed away into the harbour in front of the King's palace as undeniable evidence of what had happened, and the young man received his well-earned reward. History does not record whether the lady was worth all the trouble.

E5. TORNESS CAIRN

Two miles beyond Loch Sguabain, road and river bend sharply right at the ruins of the Torness houses, just above the Falls of Lussa, which are well worth seeing.

Halt at the falls and go across the old road to the lowest ruined building, beyond which a path leads down to the ford above the falls. One hundred and fifty yards down this path, in the low heather to the left, you will find the cairn marking the spot where the headless body of Ewen a'Chinn Bhig fell off his horse, as described in E2.

As years went by, fewer and fewer people remembered the location of this cairn, until in modern times it was known probably only to two people, one of whom was Seton Gordon the great naturalist and authority on Highland folklore, who gave me exact directions. After a long search I found the little mossy cairn deep in the heather. I have added a stone or two every time I pass until now it can be seen more readily.

Ewen's body was buried there for a few days before being carried home, and it is said that on seeing the headless body of his master, Ewen's favourite hunting hound was so shocked that every hair dropped off its body!

Ewen's ghost still haunts the Mull roads and rides furiously round the old castle of Moy, Lochbuie, before a death in the Maclaine family. (E10) Some people claim to have seen the 'Great Black Dog of Loch Buie' on such an occasion.

Beside Loch Ba, where the trees end near the mouth of Glen Clachaig, the trunk of a very old birch tree lies almost horizontal. This is where a Maclean clansman, desperately fighting off Ewen's ghost with one hand, steadying himself by gripping what was then a sapling with the other, fought for a whole night, at the end of which he had almost torn out the sapling by the roots, and the thin trunk lay almost horizontal. It still does. The man was saved by cock-crow, when the ghost vanished.

Even Sir Walter Scott knew of the Headless Horseman, for he wrote, in *Lady Of The Lake*:

> *Sounds, too, had come in midnight blast*
> *Of charging steed careering fast,*
> *Along Ben Talla's shingly side,*
> *Where mortal horseman ne'er might ride.*

Ben Talla or Talaidh (2,496 FEET) is the shapely 'sugarloaf' hill between Glenmore and Glen Forsa.

E6. PEDLAR'S CAIRN

Proceed down well-wooded Strathchoil for one and a half miles (a complete contrast to the bleak western end of Glen More), to a point where a pool in the River Lussa curves under a low bluff below the old road. It is difficult to locate the place from the new road above, which passes through Forestry plantations. Better go on to Ardura (E7), and enjoy a quiet walk up the old disused road beside the Lussa for three quarters of a mile to the Pool.

This is the 'Pedlar's Pool', beside which stands a cairn surmounted by an iron Celtic cross inscribed 'John Jones, died 1

April, 1891, aged 60 years'. John Jones was a pedlar, who, during his rounds, called at a house in the Ross of Mull where the occupants had been stricken down with smallpox or typhus. Now, that disease was regarded then with almost superstitious horror by the people, who would do little or nothing to help the victims. (A precursor, perhaps, of the fate that seems to await some of the unfortunate victims of today's plague of AIDS.) Food and drink would be left near the stricken house for the victims to collect, if they could. Bodies were coated with tar and dragged away on tarpaulins for burial.

This stranger, John Jones, was the only person prepared to nurse that family and look after the house. We do not know how the victims fared, but in due course, when Jones took to the road again, and arrived at this sheltered corner by the river, he found that he himself had contracted so virulent an attack of the disease that he died there and was buried on the spot along with his pack. The sad story of a man who gave his life for strangers.

E7. MONUMENT TO DUGALD MACPHAIL

This stands prominently beside the crossroads at Ardura, near the head of the grand sea pool where the Lussa opens out into sheltered Loch Spelve. He was the composer of what has become the Anthem of Mull, 'At t'Eilean Muileach' – The Isle of Mull – one of the most beautiful of Hebridean airs. The monument, erected in the 1920s, is built with stones from the ruins of the nearby house Derrychulin where he was born, and four verses of the song have been inscribed round the side panels and the words *'Dughall an t-Strath Chaoil – Born 1818 – Died 1887. This cairn is erected with stone from the dwelling of the bard.'*

E8. MEMORIAL SEAT, *Ardura Hill*

Fork right at Ardura for the side road to Lochbuie, eight miles distant. At the summit of steep winding Ardura Hill, among sheltered woods and a quieter countryside, there is a well and a memorial seat erected for the refreshment of weary travellers, in memory of Margaret Elliott, a local benefactor, who died in 1924.

E9. LOCH UISG

At Kinloch Spelve a road strikes left just short of the church for four miles to Crogan, another of Mull's old piers, and a small community in the peninsula of Laggan, which is, by the way, excellent deer-stalking country. At the sixth mile from Ardura, the road skirts this attractive loch which resembles more some corner of the mainland Trossachs than a district of a wind-swept Hebridean island, well wooded, backed by masses of rhododendrons. Two miles beyond, the road ends at the shore of open, windswept Lochbuie, beside a pyramidal cairn erected by 'Lochbuie and His Highlanders' to commemorate the coronation of Edward VII.

E10. LOCHBUIE

A place whose history goes far back into pre-Christian times, dominated to the north by the great bulk of Ben Buie's 2,354 feet. ('Buie' means 'Yellowish'.) Turn left along the pebbly side road above the shore for a quarter of a mile to the lodge gates. Here the visitor should seek guidance on the route to the old castle of Moy.

A half-mile walk along the shore and through the grassy dunes will take the visitor to Moy Castle standing squarely on a flat rock beside the burn. Cleared of rocks on the shore below is

Moy Castle

the channel up which the galleys were once drawn, for this was the stronghold of the MacLaines of Lochbuie, who were descended from the fourth chief of the Duart Macleans.

Access to the interior of the castle is no longer allowed because of the dangers from loose masonry. In the living room of the ground floor there is a well of pure water, which, however much emptied, refills at once to the same level.

Many romantic and historical stories centre on Moy castle and the MacLaine chiefs. You will find some of them recounted in my book *Tall Tales From An Island*. Sadly, the estate passed out of the hands of the clan – some say the estate became heavily mortgaged through gambling. Anyway, the young chief took to the Stage in an endeavour to pay the interest and redeem the mortgage. Unfortunately, he was just a few days late in meeting the deadline for paying an instalment, whereupon his creditors foreclosed and the estate passed into other hands.

Beyond the Castle, on the flat grassy land there are several stone circles, including the best example to be seen in Mull, nine stones in a twenty-two foot circle.

Here, too, stands an old family vault of the MacLaines. Note that the name 'Moy' is from 'Mach', a pram, referring to this flat area of land.

The energetic visitor can continue for three miles of rough going to explore Odin's (or Lord Lovat's) Cave, at the southern tip of the Laggan Peninsula.

The Right of Way mentioned in D9 goes from where the main road ends at the cairn beside the shore for four miles west to Carsaig. (A13, E12).

E11. GRASS POINT

Back on the main road and four miles on from Ardura, the little hamlet of Lochdonhead is seen straggling round the head of the bay. Just short of the Free Church, a road signposted 'Grass Point' branches off right, crossing a narrow arm of the sea by a hump-backed bridge.

It is a narrow, undulating road that ends in three miles at the old inn and jetties of Grass Point. Once the chief port of Mull for Oban and the mainland, and indeed the nearest point to the mainland, this was the focal point for drove roads from all over along which black cattle were driven as described earlier. Twenty thousand head of cattle were being exported in the 1820s.

From Grass Point and other landing places in this eastern corner of Mull, tracks once converged to form the Pilgrims' Way to sacred Iona, through Glen More and the Ross of Mull. Here, too, many bodies of Kings were landed for the last overland stage of their conveyance to their final resting places. (C5, D16).

Post Office mail used to be handled here for the rest of the island, and at the end of last century, the postman from Salen covered thirty miles on foot each way twice weekly with collections and deliveries. (D2).

Not so long ago, there was an inn there, and more recently a museum and tearoom, and in front of it some quaint and lifelike models of seals had been placed on the rocks. A few yards away, the proprietor uncovered a large square rock standing on what appeared to be supporting stones, perhaps a dolmen, which would be uncommon in Mull.

The jetty is still used by small ferryboats plying between Mull, Oban and the island of Lismore, and excursions can be arranged. (A17, C5, C20, CLL, D16).

E12. DUART CASTLE

Once Dowart, properly 'Dubh Aird', or Dark Headland, this is the ancestral home of the Macleans of Mull. When the MacDonalds were finally subdued and the title of Lord of the Isles extinguished, the Macleans succeeded them as the most powerful clan in the southern Hebrides. As a matter of interest, the Prince of Wales holds the title of Lord of the Isles nowadays.

Duart Castle

A mile from Lochdonhead take the side road right marked 'Kilpatrick', which is well signposted, and leads to the castle one and a half miles distant. Dating from the 13th century, it was originally a MacDougall stronghold until that clan was superseded by the MacDonalds as Lords of the Isles; and on the MacDonald's subjection to the Scottish Parliament, it passed into the hands of the Macleans.

The Macleans then found themselves heavily in debt. Weakened by its military support for Montrose in the 17th century civil war, the clan was unable to resist the greedy demands for repayment by their creditor, the crafty Marquis of Argyle, who had purchased the debts.

In 1692, the Duart lands were forcibly taken over by the Campbells – Argyll, that is – who never lost a chance to increase their lands or their wealth. In fact, the crafty Campbells were dismissed with wary contempt by the other clans in the words: 'The Campbells and their dirty sheepskins!' meaning that the first thing the Campbells did was to commit their title to any new lands to legal documents – surely a wise precaution! Such documents were made of prepared sheepskins in the old days, and hence the expression.

The other clans proudly held their lands by the sword, not by sheepskin, a mistake which was to cost them dear in later days.

Duart Castle became partly ruinous, and was sometimes used as a barracks. Last century, Torosay estate, which included Duart Castle, was purchased from the Duke of Argyll by Mr. Murray Guthrie. In 1911 he, in turn, sold Duart Castle and 400 acres of the adjoining land to Sir Fitzroy Maclean, 10th Baronet of Duart, and Chief of the Clan, who had a distinguished army record, and who lived, incidentally, to be over 100 years old. He rebuilt, restored and re-occupied the castle as the home of the Chief, which it still remains. This was the home of Lord Maclean 'of Dowart and Morvern', who died in 1990. He had been Lord Chamberlain to the Royal Household, and for a time Chief Scout.

A visit to the Castle is a MUST for all visitors to Mull, either as a first or final point of interest. There are 30 rooms built round a central courtyard in two flats, and the walls are 10 to 14 feet thick. The dungeon, too, is a centre of interest, and there is a fine restaurant adjacent to the buildings. (A13, E10).

E13. TOROSAY CASTLE

On the right side of the main

VISIT

ISLE OF MULL WEAVERS

Go down the drive of Torosay Castle, and tucked away at the end of a little lane you will find the workshop of Bob and Kathie Ryan.

They will be weaving on one of the old dobby looms and will be happy to demonstrate their craft to you. This is an unusual opportunity to observe a very old craft, and to buy tweeds, ties, travel and floor rugs, all made on the premises.

OPEN ALL YEAR IN THE GROUNDS OF TOROSAY CASTLE

Iona
(and St Columba)

THREE MILES FROM NORTH TO SOUTH, and one and a half from east to west, with an elevation of 332 feet at Dun-I, its highest point, the island of Iona is separated from the south-western tip of Mull by the mile-wide sound of Iona.

It is connected to Fionnphort, across the Sound, by a ferry service that runs frequently throughout the day. Only a few essential motor vehicles are on the island, for there are only 3 miles of passable roads. Although the ferry boat can carry a car, you are discouraged from taking a car to Iona. There are ample parking facilities on the Mull side.

Iona village, with a population of 100 or so, centres on the jetty, and the extensive church lands lie half a mile to the north. Although historically known as Icolmkill – the Island of Columba's Church – the story of Iona does not begin with St Columba. It was a centre of pagan ritual in the Bronze and Iron Ages. The influence of the earlier beliefs was still widespread when Columba landed in 563 AD, and the Christian religion, as always, adapted for itself many of the rituals and symbols of that earlier system, for example by inscribing crosses on the standing stones that were involved in earlier religious rites.

The popular impression is that Columba came to Iona to bring Christianity to the land. While this did indeed follow, missionary work was not his reason for leaving Ireland. It was, in fact, a self-imposed penance of banishment.

What happened was this. Columba was a prince of Ireland, a grandson of Niall of the Nine Hostages, and a follower of St Patrick. He had already founded one monastery and was involved in another, when a colleague, a monk named Finnian, returned from Rome with a copy of the first Vulgate Gospels ever seen in Ireland. Always a seeker after truth and simplicity, Columba was so impressed by a reading of it that he made a copy for his own use without seeking permission. In other words, he was guilty of the first recorded breach of copyright!

Detected in this unauthorised act, he was ordered to give up his copy, but even though the case was reported in the end to the High King of Ireland, Columba stubbornly refused. This was when the King made his pronouncement against Columba 'To every cow its calf, and to every book its copy'. The outcome was an armed confrontation between the two factions at the battle of Cul Dremne, and while Columba's supporters prevailed, he was overcome by the bloodshed his stubborness had brought about, and resolved to leave Ireland, never to return.

Setting out with twelve companions, he landed first on the

Garvelloch Islands – 'The Isles of the Sea' – in the Firth of Lorne. (In fact, his mother is said to have been interred on Eilean Naoimh, which lies just over thirty miles from Iona, and where Columba is said to have stayed from time to time to rest from his exacting duties.) Finding he could plainly see the hills of Ireland from there, Columba moved on, this time to Iona, where the party landed at the small bay called Port a' Churaich (Harbour of the Coracle), which lies near the marble quarries in the south.

Here his wanderings came to an end, for not even from the highest point of Iona could he see Ireland. The island of Iona had been gifted to Columba by Conall, King of Dalriada. The coracle in which Columba and his followers came to the island is described as being quite a stout craft, a framework of wood covered with tarred hides, 60 feet in length. Also according to tradition, two small stone pillars at Port a Churaich mark the length, while the coracle itself was buried under a mound, thus removing any temptation for Columba to move away. This early type of craft was clumsy to handle, and could only sail before the wind.

Around this mound there are piles of stones supposed to have been placed there as penances by the monks and as Pennant wrote, rather pawkily, in 1772 during his famous visit: *'To judge by some of these heaps, it is no breach of charity to think that there were among them some enormous sinners!'*

However, Columba's restless nature and spiritual dedication did not allow him to withdraw into monkish seclusion. There was much to do. There was a pagan people awaiting the Word, not only around him, but across in Mull and far beyond. An area of Church land was marked off – some of the boundaries can still be discerned from the air – within which an abbey was founded, and cells and buildings constructed, originally temporary structures of wood and wattle.

As time went on, the monastic craftsmen raised buildings of

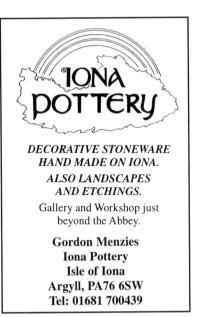

stone, with artistic ornamentation. Some of the carvings are of bizarre designs on the same principles as those in the church of Notre Dame in Paris, and the fearsome, almost oriental designs of mythical creatures, all calculated to terrify and ward off the powers of evil.

The practice reminds us of the old Scottish lady who always bowed when the name of Satan was mentioned. Reproved for this by her minister, she retorted thoughtfully, 'Ah, weel, meenister, but ye nivver ken, do ye...' The influence of the pagan beliefs seems to have lingered, if we are to believe another story connected with the building of St Oran's Chapel, which lies near the Abbey. As fast as a wall was built up, by next morning it was found flattened again. It came to Columba in a vision that only by conforming to the ancient custom of burying a living person under the foundations could the building ever be completed. He called for volunteers, and at once Oran came forward. Sadly, for he was a loved disciple, Columba had him duly interred, and the work proceeded normally. Three days later, Columba, still grieving for his lost friend, directed that Oran's face be uncovered for a farewell look. When the face appeared, the lips uttered the shattering words (translated from the old Gaelic story) 'Heaven is not as it has been written; neither is hell as commonly supposed.' Horrified by this blasphemy, Columba ordered at once 'Earth, earth in the mouth of Oran, that he may blab no more.'

The name of the pagan god of the sea is preserved in the local name *Dun Mhanannain* – the same root as appears in the name 'Clackmannan', beside the Firth of Forth. Obviously the monks must have had strong initial resistance to their early efforts to introduce Christianity.

As time went on, Iona earned the reputation of being the 'University of the North', or the 'Cradle of the Celtic Kingdom', and Columba, the 'Morning Star of Scotland's Faith'. Pilgrims came from far away seeking the teachings that flowed from Columba and his disciples. What has been called the Pilgrims' Way, marked by standing stones, stretched from the old centre of communications in the east of Mull at Grass Point (the nearest point to the mainland) and by tracks through the Ross of Mull to Iona.

During the years that followed, the bodies of kings of Scotland, Norway and France were conveyed to Iona for interment in that place of permanent sanctity: abbots, clan chiefs, even an Archbishop of Canterbury, according to Martin Martin. All were carried along the Street of the Dead, which is still preserved in parts, to the place of interment in Reilig Odhrain (Oran's Burying Place). Forty eight Scottish kings lie there, from Fergus II to MacBeth. Kenneth MacAlpin, the first king of a unified Scotland, lies there. In Macbeth, Shakespeare's historically inaccurate play, Macduff was asked where King Duncan's body lay. He replied:

Carried to Colme-Kill,
The sacred storehouse of his predecessors
And guardian of their bones.

And he was soon followed by his murderer, Macbeth himself.

It is, I think, unfortunate that the row of ancient, worn slabs that marked the traditional burying place of kings and prelates, which was once within a railed enclosure, has been removed to avoid further weathering, it is said (although any carvings were gone long since). The slabs are now displayed within the Abbey cloisters and museum. What may have been a well-meaning act has removed an item of general, sacred and historical interest, which should at least have been marked.

When that great traveller Dean Munro visited Iona about the year 1549, he found three small chapels near St Oran's Chapel, bearing Latin inscriptions, indicating that they were the tombs of Scottish, Irish and Norwegian kings. Since then, all traces have been lost of those royal tombs.

Earlier this century there was a line of 20 or 30 ancient flat slabs surrounded by an iron fence, said to be the graves of the kings. It lay a short distance south of St Oran's Chapel. There is hardly a trace of it today, which is a great pity, for it represented a significant piece of Scottish history.

Bodies of kings and nobles were conveyed across Scotland, for example to Portencross, in Ayrshire, on the Firth of Clyde, and to Corpach, the Place of Bodies, near Fort William. From such places they were carried to Iona along the shortest land and sea routes.

Quite apart from the desire to lie forever in a place of such sanctity, there was a tradition that Iona was also an island of permanent geological stability. This is brought out in the very old Gaelic prophecy translated as:

Seven years before that awful day
When time shall be no more,
A watery deluge will o'ersweep
Hibernia's mossy shore.
The green-clad Isla too shall sink
While with the great and good
Columba's happy isle will rear
Her towers above the flood

Geologists will tell you that Iona differs structurally from its younger neighbour, Mull, across the Sound of Iona. It lies to the west of a great land dislocation (The Moine Thrust) running NNE through the Sound to the Pentland Firth east of Cape Wrath. West of the line, and stretching right across the Outer Hebrides and the North Atlantic are some of the oldest rocks in the world, of which Iona is a part, probably 1,500 million years old.

Following the Celtic tradition, Aidan was pronounced king of Dalriada by Columba in 574 AD but in the new Christian manner. During his lifetime, Columba was closely associated with the royal line of the Dalriadan rulers. Christian relics have been found at Dunadd, the fortress-capital of Dalriada, in south Argyll.

Knowledge and sanctity were turned into action. Mull soon came under the influence of St Columba – in fact, some of his sayings are still current there. You will be shown the Rock at Salen, from which he once preached, and probably you will be told that 'Indeed he had not a very large congregation that time.'

He travelled extensively, carrying the Word into the land of the Picts, for the language they spoke, coming from a common root, was mutually understandable. Of course, there were other great Celtic missionaries in Scotland, such as St Ninian, St Kentigern, St Bride and St Maolruabh, the Red Saint of Applecross, some of whom had become established before Columba. The difference between them and Columba was that while their missionary work was comparatively local, Columba's was widespread.

We may well disregard much of the hagiography and legend that has gathered round Columba and the rest of the Celtic missionaries (or saints, as, in spite of Rome, they are still known), but without doubt we can still believe in Columba, the great, simple-hearted missionary to the Highlands.

Sancte Columba pater!
quem fudit Hibernia mater.
Quem Christi numen dedit Ecclesiae fore lumen.

It was when Columba was travelling to Inverness to bring Christianity to the land of King Brude, of the Picts, that the first sighting of the Loch Ness monster was recorded. Here is the story, as related seventy years after the death of the Saint, by his chronicler Adamnan, in his *Life of Columba*.

As the party approached the Ness they met a group of local people bewailing the death of one of their number who had been seized by a great water creature. Nevertheless, Columba sent a follower swimming across to fetch a boat so that the crossing could be made in comfort. The swimmer, too, was confronted and terrified by the same monster, but as it was about to seize the man, Columba approached the margin, raised his arms, and 'forbade' the creature *'whereupon it withdrew as if drawn by ropes'* and the party duly crossed in safety.

In his mighty, many-volumed *History of the Reformation*, Dr D'Aubigne wrote of Columba that:

> *He prayed and read, he wrote and taught, he preached and redeemed the times. With indefatigable activity he went from house to house, and from kingdom to kingdom. The king of the Picts was converted, as were also many of his people; precious manuscripts were conveyed to Iona, a school of theology was founded there, in which the Word was studied... Ere long a missionary spirit breathed over this ocean rock so justly named the 'light of the western world.' ...The sages of Iona knew nothing of transubstantiation, or of the withdrawal of the cup in the Lord's Supper, or of auricular confession, or of prayers to the dead, or tapers, or*

incense: they celebrated Easter on a different day from Rome; synodal assemblies regulated the affairs of the Church, and the papal supremacy was unknown. The sun of the Gospel shone upon these wild and distant shores.

There is some confusion about the nature of the Celtic (or Columban) Church, and its relationship with the Church of Rome, which was, of course, the mother Church. While adhering to the basic principles of Rome, Columba and all the other missionaries in Scotland (northern England, Ireland and Wales, too) established what is called the Celtic Church, introducing or perhaps re-introducing greater simplicity in the presentation of the Word, and conveying it in the language of the people.

The influence of the Celtic Church became widespread wherever its missionaries penetrated. Although there were no great doctrinal differences between the Celtic and the Roman churches, certain differences did appear, mostly in unimportant (to us today) matters, such as the shape of the monkly tonsure and the date of Easter. Such matters were supposed to be settled by the Synod of Whitby in the seventh century, and indeed after that the churches in Wales and Ireland clearly accepted the supremacy and guidance of Rome, but that was much less so in Scotland, where the old Celtic Church remained strong, and developed into the Church of the Culdees (Servants of God).

By the year 1144, King David of Scotland could thole this creed no longer, and he began to suppress the Church of the Culdees and restore the true format of the Church of Rome. This was the beginning of the end of the Columban Church, although not of its permanent influence, nor of the practical examples of industry and learning maintained by the monks of Iona and elsewhere throughout the Middle Ages, when they kept the lamp of civilisation burning during the dark days.

In 1203 a fine Benedictine monastery was built in Iona at the instance of Reginald, son of Somerled, the famous chief of the Clan Donald. It replaced the older building destroyed by the Norsemen. At the same time, a nunnery of the Order of the Black Nuns was also built – today it is a picturesque ruin whose crumbling walls are covered with a riot of flowers in summer.

This introduction of women to Iona would have shocked St Columba to the core. During his lifetime it is recorded that he would not allow either a woman or a cow to set foot on the island, not even the wives of the men employed as lay workers. All women had to go across to Eilean Nam Ban (Womens' Island) which shelters the little bay known as the Bullhole, below the granite quarries of Tormore, just north of Fionnphort.

What Columba is reported to have said (a saying still quoted on Mull) is:

Far am bi bo bithidh bean:
'Sfar am bi bean; bithidh mullachadh.
(Where there is a cow there is a woman;
And where there is a woman there is mischief)

It is also said that Columba banished all frogs and snakes from Iona in his desperate desire for purity, although both frogs and snakes are plentiful enough in Mull, just across the narrow Sound.

Life for the monks of Iona over the years had been anything but peaceful. In the year 806 the Norsemen, seeking the gold and treasures usually associated with religious orders, descended on Iona, plundered the place, and at what is known as the Bay of Martyrs slaughtered sixty-eight monks. Some years later, this happened again, and in 986 came the third and final raid that left so much of the work in ruins.

One story is related in connection with this raid. The raiders found the shrine of St Columba, but it contained only the bones of the Saint, instead of the treasure they were seeking. They threw the coffin into the sea, and it floated across and came ashore at Downpatrick, in Ireland, where under Divine guidance the Abbot became aware of its identity and had it interred beside St Patrick, whose work had so influenced St Columba in his early days.

Meantime, the influence of Christianity was slowly spreading to Norway, and in fact towards the end of the period when the Hebrides were under the jurisdiction of Norway, the Bishop of Iona was ordained in Trondheim. This provided some sort of protection at least for Iona, and the Norse raids concentrated more on northern England, while restless Norse, and emigrants from Norway, still raided far along the western costs of Europe and beyond.

Over the years those resilient and gifted monks created a world of art. Here, about the year 800, the magnificent Book of Kells was made, a triumph of Celtic art. The carving on the three crosses remaining on Iona, Maclean's, St Martin's and St John's, but particularly the last two, which date from about the same time, shows the influence of ancient Celtic art and Pictish designs. The quality of the work of those craftsmen influenced the designs of buildings elsewhere, such as the cathedral on St Patrick's Isle on the Isle of Man. Slates for the Abbey of Iona were brought over from the island of Luing.

But evil days were to fall on the island and its churchmen with the implementation of an Act of 1561. Under the new Presbyterianism of the Reformed Church, Iona, as a stronghold of the Church of Rome, became a target for vindictive vandalism.

The island, which had recovered repeatedly from wanton destruction by the savage Vikings, was at a stroke turned into a sacred desert by bigoted Reformers acting under direct orders from the Synod of Argyll. Buildings were 'dinged doon'; 360 crosses, it is said (probably an exaggerated figure) were smashed, removed or cast into the sea. The Abbey bells were purloined, graves and sepulchres despoiled.

But perhaps worst of all, the great library, with its treasures of art and literature, ancient Scottish records, and manuscripts by the hand of Columba himself, was burned and utterly destroyed.

Fleeing monks were able to take away with them a few of the most precious and compact treasures, which found a home in Dublin, Paris, Rome and elsewhere, but few in Scotland. Fortunately, certain items had been removed to Ireland earlier to avoid destruction by the Vikings. The Book of Kells was among them. Another was a psalter said to have been Columba's own copy of the disputed script which had brought about his banishment.

One item retained in Scotland was the beautiful, house-shaped reliquary estimated to have been made about a century after the death of St Columba in 597 AD. It is officially described as the 'Brecbennoch of St Columba'. The true Gaelic word is breachbeanachadh, meaning the 'Blessed, stippled thing'. At the battle of Bannockburn it was carried with the Scottish army as an assurance of victory, and we all know the result of that battle! After Bannockburn it was made over to the family of Grant of Monymusk, Aberdeenhire, and in 1933 it was purchased from the Grants for display in the National Museum of Antiquities in Edinburgh. It can now be seen in the Museum of Scotland.

It was also believed that certain items were hidden for safety on the island of Caimburg Mor, but were discovered and destroyed by Cromwell's troops, or by the Covenanters.

Although the Presbyterian form of worship was substituted for a time in Iona, the whole Church complex fell into decay. When Pennant visited the island in 1772, he reported that the buildings were being used as byres and were deep with animal droppings.

After the Reformation, the island came into the hands of the Macleans of Duart, and in 1693, when they fell from power

Iona Abbey yesterday

(E12), it came into the ever-open hands of the Campbells of Argyll, always ready to receive crumbs from any quarter. And there it remained, forlorn and desecrated, until 1899, when the 8th Duke presented the Abbey ruins to the Church of Scotland for restoration and use by all Christian denominations.

Certainly, in 1855, the Society of Antiquarians, in response to public feelings, took some action, but the work was poor and inadequate.

It has been quite forgotten that between 1902 and 1910 considerable restoration work was carried out by the Church of Scotland and at local level. However, the turning point came in 1938, when the Rev. George MacLeod founded the Iona Community. This dedicated body of voluntary workers was an extraordinary group. Many of them were shipyard workers from the Clyde, idle during the economic depression of the 1930s: others were University students, and others again men and women of all classes and types. These practical Christians, working during their holidays or in their sadly abundant spare time, first preserved, then slowly restored the Abbey buildings to something like their original beauty and simplicity. They were helped by gifts of cash and materials from all over the world. For instance, a valuable consignment of timber was sent from Norway, as a small recompense for the destruction caused by the Vikings. Another useful load of timber from a ship sunk during the war and washed up on the beaches of Mull was generously released to the Abbey by the Coast Guard.

In token of his energetic and devoted guidance, the sponsor of the operation was deservedly created Lord MacLeod of Fiunary in 1967.

Iona is now visited by tens of thousands of people annually. In spite of this great influx of people, even on the days when the island is overflowing with day visitors, there is always a sense of history and spirituality here for those who seek it. Even more, in the evenings and early mornings, when the day visitors have left, it is possible to experience something of the innate feeling of this ancient centre of belief.

Iona Abbey today

Once again we can share the feelings of Dr Johnson expressed in the well-known quotation: '*We are now treading that illustrious island, which was once the luminary of the Caledonian regions, whence savage clans and roving barbarians derived the benefits of knowledge and the blessings of religion... That man is little to be envied... whose piety would not grow warmer among the ruins of Iona...*'

Gone is the altar formed from a solid block of Iona marble from the quarry in the south of the island. Fishermen used to chip off a portion to carry in their boat to avert storms and danger. Gone is the Black Stone beside the Abbey where the Lords of the Isles confirmed the granting of lands. But the great Atlantic rollers still break along the dazzling, white sandy beaches on the western coast. The Fairy Knoll is still there, also known as the Angels' Knowe, where St Columba communed with the angels. There are delightful walks across green machair, bright with seasonal flowers. It is a sunny island, for the heavy rainclouds drift over to release their load on the high cool mountains of Mull.

Iona is an island of peace; in the words of Yeats, writing of another island in another land:

And I shall have peace there, for peace comes dropping slow,
Dropping from the veils of morning to where the cricket sings;
There midnight's all a glimmer, and noon a purple glow,
And evening full of the linnets' wings.
I will arise and go now, for always night and day,
I hear lake water lapping with low sounds by the shore,
When I stand on the roadway, or on the pavement gray
I hear it in the deep heart's core.

Some other books published by **LUATH** PRESS

BIOGRAPHY

Tobermory Teuchter: A first-hand account of life on Mull in the early years of the 20th century

Peter Macnab

ISBN 0 946487 41 3 PBK £7.99

 Peter Macnab was reared on Mull, as was his father, and his grandfather before him. In this book he provides a revealing account of life on Mull during the first quarter of the 20th century, focusing especially on the years of World War I. This enthralling social history of the island is set against Peter Macnab's early years as son of the governor of the Mull Poorhouse, one of the last in the Hebrides, and is illustrated throughout by photographs from his exceptional collection. Peter Macnab's 'fisherman's yarns' and other personal reminiscences are told delightfully by a born storyteller.

This latest work from the author of a range of books about the island, including the standard study of Mull and Iona, reveals his unparalleled knowledge of and deep feeling for Mull and its people. After his long career with the Clydesdale Bank, first in Tobermory and later on the mainland, Peter, now 94, remains a teuchter at heart, proud of his island heritage.

'Peter Macnab is a man of words who doesnit mince his words - not where his beloved Mull is concerned. 'I will never forget some of the inmates of the poorhouse,' says Peter. 'Some of them were actually victims of the later Clearances. It was history at first hand, and there was no romance about it'. But Peter Macnab sees little creative point in crying over ancient injustices. For him the task is to help Mull in this century and beyond.'
SCOTS MAGAZINE, May 1998

FOLKLORE

Tall Tales from an Island

Peter Macnab

ISBN 0 946487 07 3 PBK £8.99

 Peter Macnab was born and reared on Mull. He heard many of these tales as a lad, and others he has listened to in later years.

There are humorous tales, grim tales, witty tales, tales of witchcraft, tales of love, tales of heroism, tales of treachery, historical tales and tales of yesteryear.

A popular lecturer, broadcaster and writer, Peter Macnab is the author of a number of books and articles about Mull, the island he knows so intimately and loves so much. As he himself puts it in his introduction to this book 'I am of the unswerving opinion that nowhere else in the world will you find a better way of life, nor a finer people with whom to share it.'

'All islands, it seems, have a rich store of characters whose stories represent a kind of sub-culture without which island life would be that much poorer. Macnab has succeeded in giving the retelling of the stories a special Mull flavour, so much so that one can visualise the storytellers sitting on a bench outside the house with a few cronies, puffing on their pipes and listening with nodding approval.' WEST HIGHLAND FREE PRESS

LUATH GUIDES TO SCOTLAND

South West Scotland
Tom Atkinson
ISBN 0 946487 04 9 PBK £4.95

The West Highlands: The Lonely Lands
Tom Atkinson
ISBN 0 946487 56 1 PBK £4.95

The Northern Highlands: The Empty Lands
Tom Atkinson
ISBN 0 946487 55 3 PBK £4.95

The North West Highlands: Roads to the Isles
Tom Atkinson
ISBN 0 946487 54 5 PBK £4.95

NATURAL SCOTLAND

Wild Scotland: the essential guide to finding the best of natural Scotland
James McCarthy
Photography by Laurie Campbell
ISBN 0 946487 37 5 PBK £7.50

Rum: Nature's Island
Magnus Magnusson
ISBN 0 946487 32 4 PBK £7.95

Nothing but Heather!
Gerry Cambridge
ISBN 0 946487 49 9 PBK £15.00

The Highland Geology Trail
John L Roberts
ISBN 0 946487 36 7 PBK £4.99

FOLKLORE

The Supernatural Highlands
Francis Thompson
ISBN 0 946487 31 6 PBK £8.99

Tales of the North Coast
Alan Temperley
ISBN 0 946487 18 9 PBK £8.99

WALK WITH LUATH

Mountain Days & Bothy Nights
Dave Brown and Ian Mitchell
ISBN 0 946487 15 4 PBK £7.50

The Joy of Hillwalking
Ralph Storer
ISBN 0 946487 28 6 PBK £7.50

Scotland's Mountains before the Mountaineers
Ian Mitchell
ISBN 0 946487 39 1 PBK £9.99

LUATH WALKING GUIDES

Walks in the Cairngorms
Ernest Cross
ISBN 0 946487 09 X PBK £4.95

Short Walks in the Cairngorms
Ernest Cross
ISBN 0 946487 23 5 PBK £4.95

SPORT

Ski & Snowboard Scotland
Hilary Parke
ISBN 0 946487 35 9 PBK £6.99

Over the Top with the Tartan Army
Andrew McArthur
ISBN 0 946487 45 6 PBK £7.99

SOCIAL HISTORY

The Crofting Years
Francis Thompson
ISBN 0 946487 06 5 PBK £6.95

A Word for Scotland
Jack Campbell
ISBN 0 946487 48 0 PBK £12.99

LUATH PRESS LIMITED

MUSIC AND DANCE

Highland Balls and Village Halls
GW Lockhart
ISBN 0 946487 12 X PBK £6.95

Fiddles & Folk: a celebration of the re-emergence of Scotland's musical heritage
GW Lockhart
ISBN 0 946487 38 3 PBK £7.95

FICTION

The Bannockburn Years
William Scott
ISBN 0 946487 34 0 PBK £7.95

The Great Melnikov
Hugh MacLachlan
ISBN 0 946487 42 1 PBK £7.95

BIOGRAPHY

Bare Feet and Tackety Boots
Archie Cameron
ISBN 0 946487 17 0 PBK £7.95

Come Dungeons Dark
John Taylor Caldwell
ISBN 0 946487 19 7 PBK £6.95

POETRY

Poems to be read aloud
Collected and with an introduction by Tom Atkinson
ISBN 0 946487 00 6 PBK £5.00

NEW SCOTLAND

Notes from the North incorporating a Brief History of the Scots and the English
Emma Wood
ISBN 0 946487 46 4 PBK £8.99

Old Scotland New Scotland
Jeff Fallow
ISBN 0 946487 40 5 PBK £6.99

HISTORY

Blind Harry's Wallace
William Hamilton of Gilbertfield
Introduced by Elspeth King
Illustrations by Owain Kirby
ISBN 0 946487 43 X HBK £15.00
ISBN 0 946487 33 2 PBK £8.99

ON THE TRAIL OF

On the Trail of William Wallace
David R. Ross
ISBN 0 946487 47 2 PBK £7.99

On the Trail of Mary Queen of Scots
J. Keith Cheetham
ISBN 0 946487 50 2 PBK £7.99

On the Trail of Robert Service
GW Lockhart
ISBN 0 946487 24 3 PBK £7.99

COMING SOON...

On the Trail of Robert Burns
John Cairney
ISBN 0 946487 51 0 PBK £7.99

On the Trail of Rob Roy MacGregor
John Barrington
ISBN 0 946487 59 6 PBK £7.99

On the Trail of John Muir
Cherry Good
ISBN 0 946487 62 6 PBK £7.99

On the Trail of Bonnie Prince Charlie
David R. Ross
ISBN 0 946487 68 5 PBK £6.99

Luath Press Limited

committed to publishing well written books worth reading

LUATH PRESS takes its name from Robert Burns, whose little collie Luath (*Gael.*, swift or nimble) tripped up Jean Armour at a wedding and gave him the chance to speak to the woman who was to be his wife and the abiding love of his life. Burns called one of *The Twa Dogs* Luath after Cuchullin's hunting dog in *Ossian's Fingal*. Luath Press grew up in the heart of Burns country, and now resides a few steps up the road from Burns' first lodgings in Edinburgh's Royal Mile.

Luath offers you distinctive writing with a hint of unexpected pleasures.

Most UK bookshops either carry our books in stock or can order them for you. To order direct from us, please send a £sterling cheque, postal order, international money order or your credit card details (number, address of card-holder and expiry date) to us at the address below. Please add post and packing as follows: UK – £1.00 per delivery address; overseas surface mail – £2.50 per delivery address; overseas air-mail – £3.50 for the first book to each delivery address, plus £1.00 for each additional book by airmail to the same address. If your order is a gift, we will happily enclose your card or message at no extra charge.

Luath Press Limited
543/2 Castlehill
The Royal Mile
Edinburgh EH1 2ND
Telephone: 0131 225 4326 (24 hours)
Fax: 0131 225 4324
email: gavin.macdougall@luath.co.uk
Website: www.luath.co.uk